A Bond That Lasts Forever

Dawn Hubsher & Cher Hubsher

ISBN: 978-0-578-46988-1

In loving memory of Amy B. R. Gopman DMD

Contents

Introduction ♥

Women have special gifts that allow us to teach, strengthen, and express all forms of love to those that are closest to them. And no one is closer to a mother than her children. Mothers have heavenly gifts for raising children as they develop, to prepare the next generation of young girls who might choose one day to become mothers themselves. That is why the bond between a mother and daughter is so special. Without it, humankind would cease to exist.

But we weren't moved to create this book in hopes that it would increase the population! We wanted to do it because our bond is one of the most rewarding relationships in our lives. Every mother and daughter deserve to feel the kind of happiness that comes from strengthening their relationship. It means having a rock to cling to, no matter how stormy the seas are. It means having someone to call, any time, day or night, when you need someone to listen. It means knowing, in the deepest part of your soul, that no matter what the rest of the world says, someone out there loves you with their entire being.

The best part is, unless you've been forced to cut ties due to abuse or a truly toxic relationship, it's not mission impossible! We are living proof that, if you're willing to put in the work and effort, mothers and daughters from all walks of life can improve their relationships. If you wake up wanting a closer relationship with your mother or your daughter, then today is the day to begin forging that path together.

There is a famous book called *The Secret* By Rhonda Byrne, that my mom and I have read. It's about putting an idea into the universe that you want to attract into your life. The book teaches you to spend time visualizing what you want and how to move from visualization to manifesting it into existence. If you want a closer relationship with your mother or daughter, picture in your mind just what that looks like and what it would feel like. Focus on those emotions, making sure that love is the most prominent emotion of all. See in your mind the exact relationship you want to have with your mother-daughter and start putting forth the effort by taking action to create that relationship you truly want. You've already formed a great foundation by picking up this book! Now that your intention is set, continue reading for a bit of hard-won wisdom, ideas meant to challenge you and your loved one and, hopefully, a few laughs as you read about our personal experiences in between.

-Dawn Hubsher (mother) and Cher Hubsher (daughter)

So, Here's The Deal...

The only way to improve a mother-daughter relationship is to take action with love as the catalyst for that action. We urge you to take the time to read this book with your mother or daughter in the effort to strengthen your bond with each other. Discuss the chapters one at a time, and take notes either in a notebook or directly on these pages. Commit to growing together, learning together, and discussing each challenge you've faced together. Write down your own stories next to ours and reminisce over the bond and memories you two have created.

It may seem silly, but let's make it official! To further set your intentions, we urge each of you to read and sign this contract as a symbol of your commitment to one another and, more importantly, of your commitment to improving your relationship as mother and daughter:

I (mother) _____ and
I (daughter)_____
promise to commit to loving, cherishing,
and appreciating my relationship with
my mother/daughter. We promise to read this
book to learn and grow together.

Mother's Signature:

_____

Daughter's Signature:

_____

Chapter 1

From The Beginning…

❧

"A relationship like no other,
A best friend for life, daughter and mother.
Someone you can count on through it all,
A person who will be there for you anytime you fall.
The one who truly wants you to have the very best,
A relationship that makes you feel truly blessed"
By Cher Hubsher

Becoming a mother is a wonderful experience. But whether you adopt your child and have to go through that daunting and intensely emotional process, or you have a biological child, there's pain involved.

Even for those who have "easy" pregnancies, it's an intensely uncomfortable and emotionally draining experience. Some combination of cravings, nausea, vomiting, feet swelling, heartburn, back pain, crying, laughing (sometimes simultaneously) and don't even get us started on the constant invasion of privacy! By the time

1

you deliver your little bundle of joy, your doctor will be more familiar with your undercarriage than your significant other is.

All that said, no matter how easy or troublesome a pregnancy is, the moment that child is in your arms, it all takes a back seat to the joy of seeing your baby for the first time. Every morning spent on the bathroom floor slumped over the toilet in tears, every jaw-cracking contraction, every hour, week and month of waiting finally pays off.

You did it. Your baby is finally here!

And while every mother will love their child, there is also the potential for a special, wholly unique bond between a mother and her daughter that can be life-altering if nurtured properly.

It begins the moment she is born or adopted, but it must be nourished and strengthened throughout the years. More importantly, it's a bond that requires tending on both sides. As you teach your daughter to love and respect others, to always be honest, then she will emulate those characteristics and return those feelings towards you.

Creating a Strong Foundation

Creating a strong foundation with your mother or daughter is what leads to a bond that can last forever. So, what makes a strong foundation? There are a few key elements that will ensure your relationship with your mother or daughter will last a lifetime.

The first is honesty.

You create a foundation of honesty when your daughter understands she can always go to you and tell you the truth—and this is the important part—all the while knowing that, no matter how bad it is, it will not affect your love for her.

Does that mean that there aren't any consequences to her actions?

No.

Does it mean that she can keep repeating the same mistakes without fear of repercussion or reprimand?

No.

Does that mean if she wraps Dad's Corvette around a tree because she was texting and driving that you aren't going to be absolutely furious and terrified, all at once?

Of course not.

What it does mean is that she can rely on you to listen with love and empathy in your heart and to take a vested interest in helping her learn from her mistake and grow as a person rather than using her honesty against her to berate, humiliate, or punish her with the loss of your affection.

See, being honest with someone means being able to rely on them with the truth *and* the consequences. It takes a lot to confess when we've done wrong, even for an adult. If we honor our daughters when they are honest, they will continue to trust us with their truth in the future.

Think of it like putting positive energy and love into a bank. Each time we accept and love our daughters, through rain or shine, we're making a deposit. A child who is rich with love and understanding will invariably make better choices in the future, and be a happier person with a more satisfying life. Isn't that what we all want for our children?

In return, mothers need to be honest with their daughters, too. Obviously, some things are age appropriate. Should you vent to your twelve-year-old daughter that your ex-husband is a lying cheat who slept with the babysitter and that's why you're crying?

We're not psychologists but we're going to go out on a limb and say no.

But should you lie and say nothing is wrong, when it's clear that something is?

No.

Daughters need to see their mothers as people with feelings and lives beyond just them. It not only helps create a foundation of mutual respect down the line, it also teaches empathy. If mothers constantly pretend everything is perfect or put themselves last, then daughters are shown two things:

1. If my life isn't perfect like my mom's was when I was growing up, I must be broken. What's wrong with me?
2. When I become a mother, I'm to give 100% of myself over to my child and have nothing left for myself.

Neither of those things are healthy. Should a mother consider her children's needs and put them first?

Yes.

Should she only consider their needs and ignore her own self-care and well-being?

Absolutely not.

You can't constantly give from a well that is never refilled. It's important to find a balance between leaning on your daughter or expecting them to act as your therapist, and trusting them enough to see you as a real person with thoughts and feelings. In order to do that, mothers need to open themselves to their daughters in a way that maybe generations past didn't. Sometimes that means being vulnerable, and that's okay.

Of course there are some things you sugarcoat when your daughter is young, like the truth about Santa Claus or the Tooth Fairy. But the older they get, the more open you can (and should) be. This gets tougher in the teenage years, but we can promise you, it's better for them to learn about sex from you than it is to hear about it on the school bus.

And when your daughter understands you'll always be honest with her and she can trust that you won't judge or mock her for asking, then she'll come to you for the answers to some of life's hardest questions.

"You cannot get through a single day without having an impact on the world around you. What you do makes a difference, and you have to decide what kind of difference you want to make." – Jane Goodall

The second key element of a good foundation is gratitude.

Mothers have an easier time being thankful because it's a natural motherly instinct to praise our children when they have shown even the tiniest tokens of their love for us. But daughters, in turn, need to thank their mothers for everything they do for them, even if it's for something that has happened in the past. Though Mother's Day is a great opportunity to show our moms just how much they mean to us, it shouldn't be the only day of the year when we express to our mothers that we love and appreciate them. Finding different ways to display gratitude for one another is an integral part of creating and maintaining that unbreakable bond.

When we love someone with every fiber of our being, we know it within ourselves. But expressing it and showing that person you love and appreciate them through word *and* deed, is everything.

A quick morning text telling your mom you know she's going to slay today at her big work meeting lets her know she's on your mind even when she's not around.

Sending over a pot of homemade chicken soup when your daughter is under the weather lets her know that she's loved and cherished. A surprise mother-daughter spa day, not for a birthday, but just because, is another way to show you care. It is through those real, authentic intentions and actions that almost any bond can be mended or strengthened. And it's so worth it, because there is nothing more amazing than having your mother or daughter as your best friend in life.

Life Experience: Wanting A Daughter, by Dawn

I married Mason Hubsher in 1983 when I was just 23 years old. In 1985, my husband and I had our first son, Chad. We were so excited to have a boy! In 1987, we delivered our second son Grant, and that was just as joyous. I was especially happy because I knew Chad and Grant would grow up being the best of  friends. But I'd come from a family with two girls, so after I had these two little fellows, I didn't really know how to handle them. Everyone talks about how different boys can be from girls. Our boys were no exception to that rule. They came packed with never-ending energy and all of it seemed to be aimed at destroying our house and covering themselves in scrapes and bruises. My sons taught me so much about being a mother and all about having skin thick enough to deal with any havoc they managed to wreak, but I knew there was still one missing piece to our little family that would make our puzzle complete.

Growing up, we never went to a baseball game or football game. My sister and I were very much "girly-girls" and I missed that. Chatting endlessly while we brushed each other's hair, playing tea party and dress up which, no matter how hard I tried, I couldn't seem to get my boys to sign on for!

There was no doubt about it. I wanted a daughter. So, after having two sons and my chutzpah challenged, I decided that I wasn't going to have another child all willy-nilly and hope. I was going to do some research on how to get a girl this time!

My husband thought I was crazy when I told him that we were going to try for a daughter. He's a physician and he assured me in no uncertain terms that what I was suggesting was impossible, but I refused to be deterred.

I read this book called *How to Choose the Sex of Your Baby*, by Dr. Landrum Shettles to learn and understand what I could do to potentially influence the sex of my baby. The method described in the book is all natural and has everything to do with timing. I read it from cover to cover in a matter of days. It was one of the first books that I was really engrossed in reading because it seemed to be the only way to try for a girl naturally. I was afraid of trying for a girl by taking any pills or doing anything that might hurt the baby. But would I time my menstrual cycle and have sex every day up until day 11 of my cycle, and then stop in the hopes that I might get a girl this time?

Heck yeah, I would.

The principle of this method is to act based on your shortest menstrual cycle. For example, if your cycle is every 28 days, you would ovulate on day 14, so you have sex every day including day 11 and then stop 3 days before ovulation in order to have a girl.

My husband and I tried for two months using this method.

During the third month, my husband wanted to have sex on the 12th day and I told him no. Frustrated, he said, "You're never going to get pregnant." I'll always remember that because, even then, I felt my body changing and I really did feel like I was pregnant. It sounds so crazy to think a woman could sense a change so quickly, but sure enough, I soon discovered I was pregnant that month.

A quick shout out to Dr. Shettles for the great advice, and to my husband for putting out on command for those three months, even when he thought I'd lost my marbles!

"A daughter is a miracle that should always be loved and appreciated." - Dawn Hubsher

Now that I was pregnant, of course concerns for the health of my baby were the highest priority...but not too far behind came my hope for a daughter. As my pregnancy continued, I carried low in the front, just like I had with my sons. It got to the point that people I knew, and even strangers, began telling me I was having a boy and I was starting to believe it  myself. Back then, if there were no undue reasons for concern, they didn't do ultrasounds, so I had to wait it out in suspense.

I'll never forget the moment the baby was delivered and the doctor announced that it was a girl! I almost couldn't believe it and even questioned if he was sure, because I was just so excited and afraid it was a mix up. The day was August 19th, 1990, and it changed my life forever.

"A daughter is someone you can call your lifelong friend."
- Dawn Hubsher

From the second I saw Cher's face, I knew our bond would be different than the one I shared with my boys. Almost as if Cher was an extension of me. She even looked like me! This feeling was only intensified one terrifying night when Cher was a baby.

My husband and I went to my brother-in-law's wedding and I had someone babysit her. After the event, my husband and I were in a horrible car accident that completely totaled our car. Though we were able to leave the hospital that night, it was truly a miracle that we weren't seriously hurt or killed.

I came home to the babysitter telling me that Cher had cried for hours. This news was very odd because Cher was usually a very amicable baby. Sure, she cried when she needed soothing or was hungry, but crying all night and inconsolable? Never.

When I asked the babysitter when Cher had started crying, it was exactly the same time that we were in the car accident. It was like she felt that I was in danger and knew something had happened. It might seem impossible, but that sense of some tangible cord between us exists to this day.

Later in life, when Cher was in high school away on an overnight school trip for a convention, she had this dream during a nap on Christmas Day that I was going to get into a car accident right in front of the supermarket near our home. When she woke up, she was so nervous that she immediately called me to warn me not to drive in front of the supermarket, that she had this weird sense that I was going to get hit from behind and have horrible whiplash. I ensured her that there was no one out on the roads since it was Christmas Day and not to worry about it. But the very next day, I was driving by that same supermarket and, sure enough, her dream came to pass, exactly as she had told it to me.

By that point, we'd had so many little instances of this throughout our lives together, it almost wasn't even a surprise. But we've long since learned to trust those feelings and intuitions, and to make sure to share them, no matter how silly or inconsequential they seem. Better safe than sorry.

More than that, though, we've taken what was a natural connection between us, nurtured it, and given it room to grow. Having her has been one of the greatest blessings of my life.

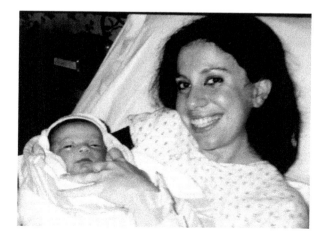

There Is No Right Or Wrong, Only Try

When a child is born, a mother isn't given instructions on how to raise her child. Instead, we simply have to go on gut instinct. Whether you choose to bottle feed or breast feed, use disposable diapers or cloth diapers, co-sleep or night train, there is no perfect answer besides doing your very best to ensure that your child is happy and healthy.

No matter where you are with the relationship you've formed with your mother or daughter, whether it's a good relationship that you want to make even stronger, or a relationship that has deteriorated over the years, now is a great time to start putting in the work. The only thing you could ever be asked to do is to dedicate yourself to trying every day, whether or not you first stumble.

If you're repairing a broken relationship, it will be difficult. But the most important thing to remember is to never give up. Having a strong relationship with your mother or daughter is worth fighting for. And again, don't underestimate small acts of caring and consideration.

Start today, right now! Maybe just with a text or phone call to see how they are doing. A card in the mail or a long email to brighten their day. An invite to lunch or dinner. Little tangible symbols of love that illustrate your willingness to sacrifice part of your day to reach out to them shows you are dedicated to them and your relationship.

Too far away for a visit? Modern technology allows us to see our loved ones through video talk. A couple of FaceTimes each week spent catching up or to share a recipe or talk to each other about day to day life is all it takes to strengthen the bond between a mother and daughter.

What you choose to do as an expression of your love and commitment isn't important. That you choose to do it is what counts. As you put forth the effort and she does the same, you'll find yourself growing closer. Honesty will flow easier between the two of you, you'll begin sharing all aspects of your life together, and you'll be able to rely on each other for the good times and the bad times.

As you continue to read this book, you'll discover the uniqueness of the special bond between Cher and I through the life experiences that we've shared. Our moments together aren't all rainbows and sunshine, but they truly demonstrate what it's like to have a strong mother-daughter bond that can overcome any obstacle that life throws at us. That said, each mother-daughter relationship is unique, and even if you didn't start out nurturing that closeness from the start, there is still time for you. Remember, it is *never* too late to create the life you've always wanted with your mother or daughter.

Now is the time to start putting forth the effort needed to create that special bond because it can truly be life-changing. The relationship you want is very possible, so long as you are both willing to try.

Now, go call your mom or daughter! We know you can do it!

"Call your mother. Tell her you love her. Remember, you're the only person who knows what her heart sounds like from the inside."- Rachel Wolchin

Chapter Objectives...

✓ A strong mother-daughter relationship is created through first trying to strengthen the bond.

✓ A strong mother-daughter foundation requires honesty, gratitude, and love.

✓ We show love through our dedication, hard work, and self-sacrifices.

✓ The smallest of actions often speak volumes.

Chapter 2

Re-enforcing That Bond Regularly

You've finally gotten your fondest wish and now you have the daughter you've always dreamed of! Now it's time to make sure you strengthen that bond whenever you can so it can continue to grow.

Children can sense very early on when they are cherished or when they are a burden. Making sure your young daughter knows that she matters and that you are willing to take time out of your day to dedicate solely to her is key. What you do with that time is almost immaterial! Whether it's something small like breakfast together before school or a bedtime story ritual, or a longer stretch of time like a weekend camping trip, take the opportunity to connect with her when you're able. Let her know that you *want* to spend time with her, and the rest will fall into place as you discover your own little traditions and fun mother-daughter activities.

Life Experience: Girls' Day, by Dawn

When Cher was just starting school, being apart so many hours a day was a struggle for her after having all my attention for so many years. I would wake her up early in the morning to help her get ready for the day, and was always met with groans or pleas for five more minutes of sleep. But, every once in a while, even though it probably wasn't the best choice as a parent, I had a special day planned that didn't involve any school bells. (I felt she was still young enough that she could afford to miss a day here or there). She would wake up thinking about her dreadful upcoming day at school, but then I would whisper in her ear, "It's girls' day! You want to play hooky?"

Cher would pop up from her bed, which she never did in the morning, just all smiles and excitement. On our normal school mornings, I would have to help dress her before she would agree to completely wake up. But when we would have a girls' day, she was like a whirlwind, jumping up and so excited to get ready. Then, off we would go to have a special day, just us two, together.

We'd go out to lunch or to a tea house, then we would go and shop till we dropped, which we still do to this day. What really made it the most fun was the fact that we were spending quality time together, and we didn't tell anyone at all what we were doing. Even my husband didn't know what we were up to until the fateful day Cher and I got busted...

It was a cool fall morning, and I'd been wanting to take Cher to this petting zoo before we went shopping because she loved animals. We went and had an amazing day drinking cider, feeding the goats and pigs, and just enjoying our time together. Afterwards, we went to a few stores and then rushed to get home before my husband and the boys got home.

Everything went according to plan, until we all sat down later that evening for dinner. I was serving up a delicious lasagna when my husband reached out and I felt a tug on my hair.

"What's this?" he asked, holding his hand out.

I looked down in shock to find a piece of straw sitting in the center of his palm.

"Gee, I don't know," I said, catching Cher's wide-eyed glance.

"Looks like a piece of straw," he said, inspecting it more closely. "Did you have a roll in the hay with someone while I was at work?" he replied with a chuckle.

My face got all hot and I started to stammer because, while I certainly hadn't been out rolling in the hay with anyone, I hadn't been totally honest with him, either. He clearly noticed my panicked reaction and then started to panic himself, his face going pale.

Dear Lord, my husband actually thought I might have been cheating on him! I had no choice. I had to come clean.

"I let Cher play hooky and we went to the petting zoo and then we went shopping!" I blurted in a rush.

Cher let out a groan as her brothers immediately started hollering in protest.

"No fair!"

"Why did she get to play hooky?"

I gently reminded them that they had taken more than one day off in the past to attend sporting events (or whatever they could've done?) with their father and this was something for Cher and I to do.

After that day, I tried to make sure I let my husband in on our plans ahead of time, but every once in a while he still reminds me about that roll in the hay…

And although skipping school and playing hooky probably wasn't ideal, having that quality time with my daughter really did strengthen our bond.

Mothers of young daughters, find that one special thing the two of you can do that doesn't get shared with anyone else (unless you get busted like we did!) You'll thank me later in life when you still have those wonderful memories to cherish.

Life Experience: Happiness Is Mother-Daughter Time by Cher

When I was a little girl, I loved playing Barbies, but I especially loved playing Barbies with my mom. Our "game format" consisted of us being best friends and going shopping where we happened to meet two guys who were brothers. And every time we met them, they asked us out for dinner and then karaoke.

After we agreed to the double date, we would finish our shopping, trying to find the perfect outfit. Once we were all decked out, the Ken doll brothers picked us up in their convertible car and took us to dinner followed by karaoke, where we would each take turns singing a song.

My mom would sing *Johnny Angel* by Shelley Fabares every single time. I was a little more adventurous and would try different things depending on my mood (and how badly I wanted to impress my Ken that night).

Week after week, month after month, we would play the same game over and over again for hours. It wasn't until recently, when my mom and I were reminiscing on memories while writing this book, that I found out that she was ready to pull her hair out some days from the sheer boredom of us playing the same game over and over.

She said she would try to change up the Barbie story that we developed to make it at least a little more fun for her to play.

"How about if Barbie is an obstetrician and we can deliver a baby?" or "How about we're cheerleaders on our way to a big competition!"

But I shot down every single idea like I was Doc Holiday and it was the Wild West.

As an adult, it's easy to see why that must have been about as fun as watching paint dry for her, but even as we cracked up over it recently, she explained that it made her happy to see me happy, and she always felt blessed that her daughter wanted to spend the time with her.

I can't thank my mother enough for going that extra mile to make me happy, even when it wasn't always a walk in the park for her.

So remember, there's no need to go rock climbing, ziplining, or skydiving to make a girl's day memorable. Simply being with one another, making memories and doing simple things can bring you even closer together.

Chapter Objectives...

✓ Find that special something, just for the two of you, that will help strengthen your bond as your daughter grows.

✓ Whatever your activity, unplug, really connect and be present.

✓ It doesn't take big gestures or lavish gifts. It just takes a willingness to commit your time to one another.

Chapter 3

Learning From the Past to Help Shape the Future

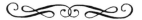

Our past is very much a part of our future. As we live a life full of happy memories and mistakes we'd rather forget, we use what we've experienced to create the future we want.

No mother-daughter relationship is perfect. But when we see each mistake as a lesson, then we never truly fail. We only learn what we can do better the next time we are presented with the same situation. History has a way of repeating itself, and you'll find yourself facing the same situations your own mother aced. It will be up to you to decide if you'll take the same path as she did, follow that path with some slight modification, or forge an entirely new trail forward...

Life Experience: Let Your Experiences Guide You, by Dawn

"Life is 10% of what happens to you and 90% of how you react to it." – Charles R. Swindoll

I grew up with parents that I love very much. They are in their mid-eighties now, but I still speak to my mom every day, and I'm there for them for whatever they need. That said, like most people, there are parts of my childhood I would've changed if I could have. Parts that have shaped me into the mother I am today and influenced how I wanted to raise my own children.

For example, in some ways, my mom was a lot of fun. She would encourage me to use my imagination. I would dress up in her clothes and strut around the house in her high-heeled shoes pretending to be a celebrity. I also enjoyed spending time with her as she taught me how to wear makeup and apply the perfect coat of red lipstick in order to make my lips look fuller. She always said, "The bigger the lips, the better the kiss". I also loved our mother-daughter ritual of going to late lunches at Chock Full O'Nuts and sitting there talking for hours.

On the other side of the coin, she's never been what you might call a "morning person". When I was younger, there were a lot of days I remember entertaining myself and waiting for her to wake up and be present. Once I had my own kids, I knew asking her for morning babysitting help was a nonstarter. She also wasn't very big on attending school functions for us, so when my kids came along, I knew that getting her to attend Grandparents Day activities would be like pulling teeth. I adapted, and attended on her behalf, instead. I was the mother for Mother's Day, and the grandmother for Grandparents Day.

As my kids grew older, they became less needy (as children do), which made my parents much more receptive to having them around. Cher remembers her poppy (my dad) attending some of her dance classes and taking her to get ice cream shakes for dessert afterward. She remembers her nanny (my mom) doing tarot card readings for her and staying up late watching reality TV together. They grand-parented their way, and had their own special moments that didn't include school functions or early mornings.

And that's *okay*!

I have accepted my own mother's limitations with the knowledge that I, as a mother, have some too! No one of us is a perfect parent. Compromise, forgiveness, and the willingness to adapt are key to keeping those mother-daughter connections healthy. Not only that? They're also key to keeping your own heart and mind happy and healthy. Festering resentment helps no one, least of all the person harboring it. My parents grand-parented *their* way, just like they parented their way. And they did a great job. But that doesn't mean I couldn't do a great job too, with some changes of my own that I felt would help shape the bond between me and my kids in an even stronger way.

For example, the lack of that presence at school activities in my own childhood resulted in me making the very active choice to be involved with my own children and *their* school activities. I may have even gone a little overboard (if you consider attending all five showings of a spring musical "overboard", which I don't.)

When it came time to volunteer for room mother, or field trip chaperone, you better believe my hand was up! Did someone say six dozen cookies for the bake sale...by tomorrow???

Count me in.

Is that the right path for everyone?

Certainly not.

With time such a precious commodity these days, we all have to pick and choose what we can do with and for our kids. This was my choice because I knew it was something I'd have appreciated in my youth and something my own daughter really appreciated. Maybe having a parent at school functions isn't important to your child, but attending their sporting events is. Or maybe they'd rather have you to themselves for a weekend camping excursion over having you be president of the PTA. **The point is, you don't have to be Super-Mom to be a super mom.** You just have to do your best to be present for your kids when they need you most. And the best part is? You get credit for trying, even when you don't always succeed. Because nobody is perfect!

Another issue I had when I was a child was that I never understood why I never went on trips with my parents. My parents traveled many weekends, but it was always just the two of them. I would sometimes ask why we would never go away as a family, and their answer was always, "When you are older, you can travel." Off they went, while my sister and I stayed with our grandparents.

Don't get me wrong. Those were some of the best days of my life. And maybe that was part of why my parents did it. They knew we'd spend a couple of days being doted on by two of the people who loved us most. And, man, my nanny and poppy were the best. They always had a new special toy for me when I got there. And every Friday night, we would bake a cake from scratch and watch the oven as our mouths watered until it was finally time to eat it. They would help us with our homework, take us for ice cream bonnets on our Saturday afternoon walk, and sew clothes for our dolls. Every Saturday night, my sister and I would perform a skit for them as they applauded us and encouraged us to be the best we could be. Then, every Sunday night, they would give us a bath and wash and dry our hair before sending us home with our parents.

Now that they're gone, I miss them every single day. When I become a grandmother (I've already put in a request with "management" to be called "Mimi") I really hope to be just like them. I always felt wanted and supported when they were around and they always made me feel loved.

But there was always a part of me that wondered what I was missing when my dad wasn't stressed out from working so hard and got to unwind and relax…what they got to see and experience on those trips that we didn't.

I decided when I became a wife and a mother, I would still go on trips with my husband alone occasionally, but the majority of our travel would be done as a family. These vacations are some of our best memories, and definitely brought us closer together as a family. I wouldn't trade them for the world.

"Family time is the best time." - Carmelo Anthony

Was I traumatized by missing out on weekend vacations with my parents? Of course not! Did I want my daughter to be able to experience travel as a child? I did. I adopted what worked and really analyzed what didn't, and created my own parenting style. There are no rights or wrongs here. Just choices that we, as mothers, have to make each day.

But Mistakes Happen

Sometimes, though, there are parenting decisions that have much longer-lasting ramifications on our kids. Ones they never really forget…

As a child, I always had hard-to-manage, curly hair. Rather than deal with detangling it and styling it, my mother often got fed up and opted to cut it into a pixie style. And each and every time, I would cry.

Bitterly.

Afterwards, my mother always felt bad and would tell me that I never had to have my hair cut so short again. But life got in the way, and a few frustrating braiding sessions later, I'd be back in that chair trying to hold back the tears. Oh, how I hated having short hair. Strangers would call me "son", and kids would tease me because I looked like a boy. I even took to wrapping towels around my head and pretending it was my long, beautiful hair.

Around the time that I was eleven, I finally let my feelings be known and asked my mother to sign a note promising she would never have my hair cut short again. Thankfully, she kept her word. To this day, I've never had short hair again. When I do go to the hairdresser for a trim, it's still a nerve-wracking experience for me. My hairdresser even knows to show me the back of my hair in the hand-mirror as she's cutting to reassure me. Later, my mother acknowledged that she had made a mistake. From her view, she was saving me (and herself) hours of what seemed like a thankless task, plus the pain that came along with trying to fight a brush or comb through that thick head of hair.

I understood her reasoning and forgave her, but it very much affected the way I treated Cher's hair. She had unruly hair that was even harder to manage than mine. Sometimes it would take up to an hour to brush out her hair after a bath because the curls would become so tangled and the two of us might wind up in tears after a particularly tough knot. But I made the conscious choice to help her take really good care of it, even though it was often a bit of a trial, because I didn't want her to be forced to cut her hair the way I had been.

Was my short hair the end of the world?

No.

But it made it hard for me to feel confident and good about myself. My mother's mistake had real-world ramifications that still affect me today. If I knew that, went forward and did the same with my own daughter, then I would be creating a cycle that really needed to be broken.

My advice to you is to pull up those memories. Even the ones that hurt! Not so you can let them eat away at you, or to rub your own mother's face in them. But so you can use them, both the good and the bad, to guide you. They're priceless when it comes to informing your own parenting decisions!

I used the best parts of my mother's parenting style, analyzed the parts that made me unhappy as a child, and used them to blaze my own trail. One that has shaped me into the mom that I am today and, according to Cher, the very best!

In case you needed a reminder though?

No one is perfect...

Life Experience: An Unforgettable Mistake, by Cher

My mom is awesome. And, as usual, she's SO right! There are some mistakes that stay with us forever, long after we've extended forgiveness for them...

Ever since I was 6 years old, I've always taken dance lessons. My mom felt it was good for the body and a healthy exercise. She also wished she could be a dancer but her mom would never enroll her in dance classes, so she wanted *me* to be a dancer. I started taking tap, jazz, ballet, point, hip-hop, lyrical, and modern. If you can think of it, I was doing it.

I even joined a competitive dance team and would compete all around Florida. I remember one time I even won first place for a duet I competed in and won a $250 check and a trophy. Back then, $250 was a big deal! It was a lot of fun, and I have so many great memories of that time.

At one point, though, the dance company was opening up a competitive singing division. I never took singing lessons in my life but always loved to sing. Mostly into a brush in front of a mirror.

Every year, though, my family and I would take a cruise and the kids would put on a talent show. My go-to talent was always dancing and singing 'Oops, I Did it Again' by Britney Spears.

Embarrassing?

Probably.

Fun?

Definitely.

I would go all out, dancing my little booty off. Apparently, it was pretty cute, and when auditions came around for the competitive singing team, my mom wanted me to audition with the same song and dance, complete with the snazzy step-ball-change into a split at the end.

In *my* mind, there was no way I was going to go in front of a ballet school and perform Britney Spears. Not only would it be embarrassing, but I was pretty sure I wasn't a good singer, despite my mother's assurances that I was the next Cher in the making.

I used my own judgment and comfort level and wound up auditioning with just a dance. Afterward, my mom picked me up and asked if I auditioned to sing, too. I told her, "No, of course not." She couldn't understand why I hadn't done it. We got in a huge fight that resulted in her driving me back to the auditions, marching me inside and essentially forcing me to sing.

Still swiping tears off my face, I sucked it up, popped my Britney Spear's CD in, and sang and danced my little heart out to the song, ending with the crowning glory.

A step-ball-change into a split.

And I got back crickets. Not one of the judges even clapped. I can still remember the bewildered looks on their faces as I slunk out of the audition hall, *so* embarrassed and humiliated, I felt like I wanted to crawl into a hole and die.

Needless to say, I did not make the cut and will forever consider this as the most embarrassing moment of my childhood.

Is it the worst thing ever?

No.

Ricky Townsend pooped his pants at recess one time, which resulted in people calling him "Sticky Ricky" for…well, forever. I think people still call him that! And one time this kid in my kindergarten class bent over and split his pants. Hey, at least a whole classroom full of people hadn't seen my humiliation!

But those were accidents. The thing that bothered me most was that mine was avoidable. The result of being forced to do something I didn't want to do. Even though I had fantasies of being a singer when I was caterwauling in front of the mirror with a hairbrush, throwing me into an audition which I was totally unprepared for only made me never want to sing again. I can't even go to karaoke without having flashbacks.

This was my "short haircut" moment. I had two options. I could let it fester, hang on to it, and let it affect my relationship with my mom. Or I could forgive, take note to remember how I felt in that scenario for when I become a mom myself, and make sure I don't make the same mistake with my own daughter.

I choose the latter.

Chapter Objectives...

- ✓ When we see every mistake as a lesson, then we never truly fail.

- ✓ No matter how you grew up in your family, you develop your own personality and way of doing things.

- ✓ Each mistake of the past is a life lesson that we can learn from.

Chapter 4

Grudges Are Heavy,
So Why Hold Them?

The previous chapter on making mistakes and choosing not to repeat them is a great lead-in to our next topic, which is the damaging practice of holding grudges.

A grievance is defined as 'a real or imagined wrong or other cause for complaint or protest, especially unfair treatment'. The most notable aspect of this definition is the fact that grievances are sometimes an imagined wrong. Meaning, the person wronging us didn't intend to cause any offense, but we took offense anyway.

Like in the case with the Britney Spears audition! Forcing the issue wasn't intended to hurt anyone, despite the result. In that instance, it's still better to tell the person who caused us harm how their words and actions impacted us rather than holding it inside. It's not only the best way to avoid it happening again, but it can bring you closer together once the injuring party understands the pain they've caused, no matter how unintentional.

But what about the other type of grievance? One that comes from intentional, 'unfair treatment'. We like to think that everyone we meet has good intentions one hundred percent of the time. As we go on in life, though, we learn one way or another that isn't always the case. For whatever reason, there will come a time where someone will be mean to us. They will say or do something to purposely hurt our feelings. If the offense is coming from someone close to us, it's going to hurt even more. And no matter how strong your bond is, at least once in our lives, our mother or daughter is going to say something out of anger, fear, hurt or worry that is going to wound us.

One of the hardest life lessons to learn is to get past those things. When we are hurt by our mother or our daughter, it can fester if we don't take steps to correct and heal that hurt.

So, how do we honestly get over it when someone we love has offended us or done something to hurt us intentionally?

Step One: Take a minute.

Instead of lashing out in kind or reacting in anger, separate yourself as best you can, and be the one to diffuse the situation with a little space. That could be all that is needed to start the healing process. Maybe you won't even have to contact your loved one to explain your hurt. They might have used that time to reflect and realized their mistake on their own. You might get an apology and an explanation without having to ask for either one.

If not, after a period of cooling down and when you feel

ready to express yourself without bitterness or anger, be the bigger person and reach out. It always helps to remember, despite the hurt, you're not laying yourself at the feet of your enemy. This is the person who knows you best and loves you deeply and vice versa. The only way to let go of the negativity caused by someone we love is to find a way toward forgiveness and understanding.

Step Two: Give the grace you would hope to receive.
One thing that helps us achieve the sometimes difficult task of letting go of grudges is to remember that the shoe will invariably be on the other foot someday. Maybe tomorrow you'll be pre-menstrual and the corner store will have run out of your go-to favorite flavored coffee, and you won't be able to get a cab, and you'll be late for your meeting and, just when you're about to explode with pent-up hormonal rage, your mother will stop by and make an innocent, "You look tired" comment and wind up becoming the undeserving recipient of your wrath. When you have to slink over to her house the next day and apologize, do you want her to rub your face in it and make you feel crummier than you already do, or do you hope she forgives you and remembers that *most* of the time, you treat her with love and respect?

How about when you've spent your morning running around town picking up your husband's dry-cleaning, making dinner for your elderly neighbor because his wife broke her hip, and have taken the time to stop by your daughter's office to bring her lunch and she just wrinkles her nose and asks why there are pickles on her sandwich and you literally lose it on her and tell her she's ungrateful and entitled. It's only after you get home that you realize you were overtired, had overextended yourself, and took it out on her. Do you want her to hold it over you and remind you that you called her entitled and ungrateful, or do you want her to truly accept your apology and let it go?

Grant the grace you would hope to receive if the situation were reversed. You'll thank us for it later.

The next step is what most of us find the most difficult.

Step Three: Forget it.

We know, we know. Impossible, right? But we don't mean we all have to find one of those Men in Black memory zappers to erase the instance from our minds if we want to be a good mother or daughter. What we mean is let it go. Don't bring it up again in conversation, in a text, or phone call. Because if you keep bringing up the offense in conversation and weaponizing it against your loved one, then have you honestly forgiven?

The answer is no.

Life Experience: Lightening My Load, by Dawn

Accepting criticism can be hard to take, even when it's the constructive kind. Who wants to have their flaws pointed out?

Not this lady.

Sure, sometimes that criticism can come in the way of friendly advice. Other times, though, it comes quite unexpectedly and from a person who doesn't have your best interests at heart. One of my biggest faults is that I hold grudges if someone does me wrong and I can't let it go. It nags at me and I can't seem to clear my mind of the negative things that were said or done to me.

Cher, on the other hand, never holds grudges. It was something she really trained herself to do as an adult, and I admire her for that. She explains that it takes you down a level when you hold grudges, and you use energy fussing over what the person said that could be better used in another, more positive way. Like we've said in the past, we only have one life to live, so why spend time on negativity?

That is something Cher's husband taught her. He always says, "What is the point of holding a grudge because the only one experiencing that negative feeling and energy is yourself?"

He's right. Whenever we hold a grudge, we are the ones that are in pain.

I like to think I had a little something to do with that, too, though. See, when Cher was younger, it wasn't always that way. In fact, one time when she was in her early teens, we got into a big fight on the phone while I was at work. I honestly can't even recall what it was about now, but I remember I said something that hurt her feelings. I knew it the second it came out of my mouth, but before I had a chance to apologize, she hung up on me.

Her mother.

After I carried her around in my belly for nine months, gave up wine, cold cuts, coffee and the ability to leave the house without wearing a bra.

She hung up on me.

I was livid. We'd fought plenty of times, but she'd never pulled that on me before. So I called her back about twenty times, ready to read her the riot act. And still, she didn't answer.

Full of unresolved feelings—both remorse and anger—I left work and drove home, intent on getting her to talk it through with me, and on the way there, I hit a pothole, blew out my tire, and wound up doing a 180 and facing traffic in the wrong direction.

It was only by the grace of God that I didn't get hit and managed to move the car before something terrible happened.

Now, we all know that if something did happen, it wouldn't have been Cher's fault. Or even mine, really. Sometimes an accident is just that. An accident. But what it did do is make us both realize that hanging up the phone (or going to bed, or leaving the house) angry at someone you love is a bad idea.

What if you're angry and need space?

Take the time you need. But take it after you tell your loved one, "Look, what you said really hurt my feelings and I need a little while to process it all and then we can talk. I love you."

Because accidents do happen, and you don't want the last thing you remember of your loved one to be that you hung up the phone on them.

It's something I still have to make a conscious effort to do every day, though. Whenever I start to fall back into the old pattern of holding a grudge, I try to remind myself of that day, as well as the quote that has been attributed to Nelson Mandela.

"Holding a grudge is like drinking poison and waiting for the other person to die."

Do I want to fill my body with that mental poison? I truly don't. And I certainly don't want to poison my relationship with my daughter.

So Cher and I choose to forgive *and* forget, no matter how hard it is sometimes.

"Mothers of daughters are daughters of mothers and have remained so, in circles joined to circles, since time began."
— Signe Hammer

The Feeling Of Forgiveness: Mending Broken Relationships

There are times when we come across a mother-daughter relationship that has been damaged so long ago and so deeply that the wounds seem impossible to heal. We can usually trace the cause of such damage from pent-up hurt and emotions that finally were let loose in a barrage of furious words meant to cause pain. And they do their job very well. Each insult like a piece of shrapnel to the heart, death by a thousand cuts.

Both sides drag their battered bodies to their own little corner to lick their wounds, remembering each insult they heard but forgetting the ones they hurled in return.

Only, the wounds never really heal without the proper

medicine. Instead, they grow into deep, jagged battle scars as they're opened over and over again. Silence between you reigns supreme because you have too much pain or pride or combination of both to be the one to call, and suddenly a week turns into two and then ten and after a while, it simply becomes your new normal. Before you know it, a decade has passed since you've last talked to or seen your mother or daughter.

We're here to tell you that, no matter how much time has passed since the mother-daughter relationship broke down, there is *always* a way back to mending that bond if both parties truly want it. Regardless of what has been said, what either person has done, or the number of weeks, months, or even years that have passed since there was a single word uttered between the two of you, there is still time to recreate what was destroyed. Someone just has to be willing to take that first step.

For most things, thinking something through is the best course of action. In this case, we're betting you've already thought about what you would say if you spoke to your mother or daughter. You've already imagined the varying outcomes a thousand times. This isn't the time for caution or second-guessing because that will lead you right back to where you've been; Paralyzed by fear or indecision while another year goes by where you both miss out on that relationship.

So our advice? Rip it off like a bandage. Don't think about it, don't plan every possible outcome. Just count to three, pick up the phone, and make the call.

If they don't answer the phone? Don't give yourself the out and hang up. You've done the hard part by making the call, follow it through. Leave a detailed message. Tell them you just want to talk with them, that you miss them and love them. That you *do* want to fix what was broken, regardless of how long ago it was. Don't bring up what happened or how it made you feel. Just start with the honest truth. That you want to try.

Is it going to work?

The truth is, we have no idea. But what we can tell you is that, if there is even a chance to repair that relationship and you don't take it? You'll regret it for the rest of your life. Because one day, one of you will be burying the other, and there are no take-backs then. Don't wait until it's too late.

"A daughter without her mother is a woman broken. It is a loss that turns to arthritis and settles deep into her bones." – Kristin Hannah

Life Experience: Stopping Grudges Before They Even Start, by Cher

Mending fences is great and we highly recommend it, but you know what's even better?

Not breaking the fence in the first place!

Remember earlier in the book where my mom talked about keeping my hair long even though it could be taken care of easier when it was shorter? How her actions as a mother were shaped by the negative experience she had as a child with her own mother forcing her to have short hair? Well, there is another side to that story I wanted to share.

The part that my mom missed in her version of events is that she actually did to me the same thing her mother did to her, only in reverse. Because of her traumatic hair experience, she forced me to have long hair my whole life, even though I went through several periods that I really wanted to try out a short cut. It was in style at the time and so much easier to manage. I would *beg* over and over again to cut my hair, and even wrote her notes explaining why I wanted short hair and how it was unfair, but she refused to budge.

She would say, "You will regret it and I don't want you to go through what I went through."

The flaw in her logic?

I *wanted* short hair. Especially in my early teen years.

While my mother was trying to save me the trauma of being forced to cut my hair, she unwittingly continued the cycle by forcing me to keep mine long. I know she meant well, however, this wasn't what I wanted at all.

The takeaway here isn't to bring it up and punish my mother for her decision. She knows I've long since forgiven her and it's not something I ever bring up. I do so now only to illustrate that the best way to stop someone from holding a grudge is to communicate and listen to one another. If you make that a priority in your relationship, you can stop the grudge before it even starts. Sure, maybe hair is superficial, but it can really affect a girl or woman's confidence level. So listen to what your daughter wants, even if the hair cut comes out bad. If something goes wrong, it's okay because the great thing about hair is that it always grows back! Even better, though, she'll know that you hear her, her voice matters, and you trust her to make some decisions on her own. Those lessons will benefit her far more than long hair ever will.

No matter the wrong you've experienced in your life, no matter the unexpected turn of events or the negativity that has found a way into your family, try to recall those good times. Call on the happy memories you've "banked" as mother and daughter and let them guide you toward mending the broken relationship. Arise from the ashes of that fire as new, stronger women who can take on the world together. The freedom and relief you've longed for is possible, but you have to take that first step.

We know you can do it! You can create the mother-daughter relationship you have dreamed of, regardless of what has happened in the past. But you have to start by taking that one, first step, and there's no better time than the present!

Chapter Objectives...

✓ Words are something you can never take back, and words said in anger are ones that can haunt a person for years to come.

✓ If you hold a grudge against your mother or daughter, then you'll never allow yourself to move forward.

✓ Except in cases of violence or extreme toxicity, a relationship with your mother or daughter will be worth the effort and the struggle to mend the bond.

✓ The best way to deal with a grudge is to prevent it from forming in the first place.

✓ Regardless of what life has brought you, start now to make things right — to rid your life of negativity, grudges, and long-felt hurt.

✓ Taking action is the key to sustaining and strengthening any mother-daughter relationship regardless of when the relationship starts in life.

Chapter 5

Teaching And Guiding

Mothers take pride in the things they are able to teach their daughters. There is almost nothing better than seeing our daughters excel in the areas we've helped them in. Whether it's learning their first words, teaching them the alphabet, or helping them prepare for a math test, there are many different ways that a mother will be a teacher as the daughter grows and experiences the world on her own.

That said, there is one character trait that any mother will agree a daughter needs to have to live her best life, and that is kindness.

Your daughter can be fluent in French, excel in Algebra, have the voice of Alicia Keys and the body of Heidi Klum, but if she isn't kind, you've dropped the ball.

While some people think that traits like this are inherent and can't be learned, we're going to call BS on that. Are children more inclined to be kind and empathetic? Absolutely. But, aside from the occasional sociopath, can all children be taught kindness by example?

You bet they can.

And here are some great tips on how to do it!

Practice what you preach. Telling your daughter to be kind is great, but if you follow it up by screaming at the waitress because your salmon is overcooked, you need to reexamine what you're actually teaching her.

Treat others as you would want them to treat *your daughter*. We all know the Golden Rule, but we're asking you to step it up a notch and take it even further. If your daughter was that frazzled waitress, not only would you refrain from yelling at her over a piece of fish she assuredly had no hand in cooking, you might even take a stand against someone who did! Let your daughter see you be strong, brave, and **proactive** with your kindness.

Encourage empathy. As much as you want to shield your daughter from the pain in the world, it's also important for her to see that not everyone is on equal footing. During the holiday season, gift-giving is great, but don't be afraid to let her know that other kids might not be receiving gifts this year and suggest sharing one of hers. Or make a day of it, and go shopping for toiletries and items you can make into gift bags for a battered women's shelter.

There are a million ways you can model empathy and kindness for your daughter, in addition to using your words, and we guarantee every single one of them will benefit not only the people you're extending these kindnesses to, but also you and your daughter.

Consider helping your daughter become an 'includer'. What

this means is that no matter what, regardless of any characteristic of the other person, she will find a way to be proactive in her kindness and make an effort to include them. This can mean inviting who some kids call the 'loser' or 'nerd' to sit with her at the lunch table when they have no one else to sit with. It can mean just going out of her way to offer a smile and a kind word to the people at school that the majority have shunned for one reason or another. It could also mean including them in school projects, sports, or by simply being a friend.

Model that inclusion mentality for her as well, by encouraging your daughter to invite her new friend to your house after school one day. Show her that she can make space for people who might need a friend in your shared home, and in her life, but also in her heart.

We promise you won't regret it.

"This is how we heal the 'mean girls' culture: we hold, we include, we love, we empower, and we regard our girls. And we model this in how we treat other women."
— Lisa McCrohan

Life Experience: Sometimes The Daughter Can Be The Guide, by Cher

Growing up, I always wanted to have a farm, as I've always loved animals. When I was 12-years-old, we moved into a home with a large backyard. Our neighbors had pet goats, chickens, cows, and horses. It didn't take me long to fall in love with (and personally name) every single one of them. I even begged my parents for a pet goat or lamb. Heck, I was desperate. I would've taken a weasel. I just wanted to have a pet so badly.

After a lot of begging, I was finally allowed to get a chicken. I named her Snickers and I was crazy about her. I realized pretty quickly that she was lonely when I wasn't outside with her, so my parents let me get another one, and I named her Rocky. I absolutely loved having chickens as pets, and I took great care of them.

Since my parents knew how much I adored goats, and they saw my devotion to Snickers and Rocky, they got me two goats for my next birthday, a Nubian and a Pygmy.

They were so cute. I named the goats Billy-Jean and Raffey-Mo. I was in love, and so thrilled with my little menagerie.

One evening, our family was having chicken for dinner. BBQ chicken wings and chicken tenders had always been a favorite of mine, but then it hit me:

How could I eat chicken if I had pet chickens? The ones who had died for this meal were no different than Snickers and Rocky!

In that moment, it just didn't make sense that I would eat the very same type of animals that I loved like part of my family.

I'd learned firsthand how many emotions chickens actually have. Snickers was a real character, always excited to see me and not afraid to show it. And Rocky, bless her heart, was sweet and cuddly. She loved when I rubbed her chest feathers and would almost coo as I stroked her.

I had to tell my mother that I couldn't eat dinner, and that I wouldn't eat chicken ever again.

My mother was obviously concerned and urged me to eat, but I literally couldn't bring myself to do it. I tried to reason with her and she grew more frustrated, until I began to sob at the dinner table. I wasn't budging.

I made the decision then and there, at 12-years-old, to become a vegetarian even before I knew what it really meant to be one. All I knew is that I couldn't eat animals anymore.

My mother struggled with this in a big way. She argued that since I was petite, I needed the protein from meat in order to grow and be healthy, but I persisted.

It took a while, but eventually my mother started to compromise with me when she realized how serious I was about it. If I agreed to at least eat turkey during Thanksgiving, she would let me off the meat-hook, so to speak, the rest of the time. (I said I would, but never did, at least it got her off my back for a while.) And that was good, because, honestly, I think I would've starved myself otherwise. I was going to stand up for what I believed in, which was something she had taught me.

"The mother-daughter relationship is the most complex."
— Wynonna Judd

Looking back, I know how hard it was for my mom to cook dinner every night for our family, which consisted of my two older brothers and my father with big appetites, and then have to cook a special dinner for me every time. What was even harder was the fact that neither of us knew all that much about being a vegetarian.

In the end, I wound up eating a lot of microwavable dinners that were considered vegetarian as my family ate what my mother had cooked that evening. I knew it was easier for everyone that way and it would take the stress away from her having to figure out a meal for me every evening.

Eventually, though, she admitted that wasn't a great solution, either. Together, we researched and found out what it truly meant to be a vegetarian. My mother was interested in knowing how to make nutritious meals for me that would still have plenty of protein, and I wanted to understand what I would need to eat in order to remain strong and healthy. I knew at first that my mother was so against the idea of me being a vegetarian because of my size, but eventually we were able to work together and balance the need to have me consume healthy food with my own personal beliefs.

My mother admits now that, instead of getting upset when I first told her about wanting to become a vegetarian, she wishes she would have just looked into alternative protein sources that we could've learned to cook together.

It was not until this 'phase' had clearly become a lifelong commitment, a couple of years in, that my mother started to really look into what a vegetarian was, and what it meant to me in my life. For so long she was against it, but that was because she didn't understand that being a vegetarian can actually be healthy.

Fast forward to today and I am now a full-on vegan. More shocking, though? My mom is a vegetarian! She was so impressed at how healthy I was and saw how happy this lifestyle made me that she allowed herself to be open enough to watch some of the documentaries that had inspired me. This is now something we are proud to do together.

I would never judge someone else for their eating choices, but having a mom who is open to teaching her daughter as well as learning from her? That's a win/win!

It took time to come to this new understanding, but looking back, I am so proud of myself for sticking to what I believed in and taking the opportunity to be the one guiding instead of taking a back seat and allowing her to guide me in a direction I knew wasn't right for me.

I knew in my heart that once my mom really understood my reasonings, and once she was really able to listen, she would embrace it.

And I was right.

"My mother wanted me to be her wings, to fly as she never quite had the courage to do. I love her for that. I love the fact that she wanted to give birth to her own wings."
– Erica Jong

Chapter Objectives…

✓ A mother should guide her daughter both in word *and* in deed.

✓ Kindness and empathy are key.

✓ An includer is someone who is able to create space for people in their homes, in their lives, and in their hearts for others to feel loved and included just as they are.

✓ Mothers, recognize that there is a time to teach your daughters and a time to learn from them.

Chapter 6

Compromise Creates Memories!

There is nothing we enjoy more than sitting around the table with a good cup of coffee, reminiscing about our favorite times together or funny things that have happened in our lives.

In order to create those memories, you've got to put in the time and effort. Whether it's cooking that massive Thanksgiving dinner together that didn't quite turn out as expected, or that birthday cake that nearly burned the house down. Whether it's playing Monopoly every Friday night, knowing your mom is going to make you pay through the nose for Park Place if she gets her hands on it, or braiding your daughter's (too!) long hair.

Memories are what sustain us when the person we love isn't nearby, so make a lot of 'em, and make 'em count.

But have you ever considered that, in order to do so, mothers and daughters have to make some real compromises through the years?

Do you think most moms are just getting home from work or just finished making dinner and are in the midst of doing the dishes and DYING to play Candyland, or Barbies at that very moment?

We're going to guess probably not. But when they choose to compromise, they open the door for a memory to be made or a story to be told. And while that might not have been what they wanted to do right then, those memories of playing are worth their weight in gold.

On the flip side, do you think most daughters want to go on that blind date with Lois's cute pediatrician son, sight unseen? Probably not, but by doing so we create not only goodwill with our mothers, but also create an opportunity for a memory to be made or a story to be told. Something that seemed like such a drag (or compromise) at the time can be something you laugh over for decades to come...

"When I asked him his favorite hobby, he said he likes to break things. And after dinner, he took out his calculator so he could divvy up my part of the bill. Thanks, Mom, he's a great catch!"

Does that mean that you have to do everything your mother or daughter asks you to do all the time? Nope! You have priorities and things that are important to you, and sticking to your guns or saying no sometimes is key to your own happiness. But do you have to compromise sometimes? You sure do. Relationships require it to flourish.

If you're lucky, those compromises will work out to where everyone feels great about them. If not, hopefully, at least, you'll get a good story out of it!

Life Experience: A Most Successful Compromise, by Dawn

When Cher was getting ready to enter middle school, she wanted to leave the private school system and go to public school.

To be blunt, I didn't want her to go. It was more than just the fact that Cher has a petite frame and kids just seem to get meaner and rougher the older they get. It was also the fact that I had dealt with my share of bullies in public school, myself, growing up. I was considered a 'nerd', I only had one good girl friend, and I was often picked on by the other girls because my clothes didn't quite fit me right and I unfortunately had bad acne. I was even afraid to walk home and be harassed by the other girls.

In my mind, when it came time for Cher's schooling, I figured if her father and I were paying for her to be there, we'd have a lot more say in how much of that nonsense we were willing to put up with. It gave me some sense of control, even if it was only in my mind.

As I talked to Cher more about why she wanted to try public school, I came to discover how unhappy she was at private school, and had been for many years. Cher explained that because she was so small, the other girls would talk to her in a baby voice. She even told me about a kid who cut a piece of her hair off.

The more I talked to her about her concerns, the more I came to realize that private school wasn't as controlled as I thought. It took everything I had not to take my earrings off, find those kids' mothers and show them what an angry mama bear was capable of!

I'm usually a really nice person, but I was pissed.

Not to mention, private school was a known factor. All of the families whose children attended the school were very close, the classroom sizes were smaller, and it was true that Cher was entering the age group where other kids tend to be meaner. Even though Cher was having issues of being bullied at the private school, I was certain that it would be worse for her at a public school where the classroom sizes were much larger, leaving the teachers with more students to corral. I was at a complete loss of what to do because I knew what my daughter wanted and what she had experienced. But I also feared what might happen if I did send Cher to a public middle school.

I finally bit the bullet and decided I would allow Cher to give public school a try to see if it would really make a difference. Rather than telling her no, I was willing to work with her instead of just putting my foot down as a mom and doing what I thought was the best.

But, if I found out that she was still being bullied about her size or for any other reason, she would agree to go back to private school without giving me any hassle.

About three months into her first school year at the public middle school, it was clear just how much Cher loved it. She was making new friends, she didn't have any trouble with mean girls bullying her, and her academic scores improved! It was such a wonderful experience that taught me as a mother how important it is to take the time to listen to your daughter, to honestly hear what she is saying, and be willing to compromise with her even if you are worried about making any big changes.

I also had to remind myself that Cher is not me, and just because I had a poor experience in public middle school did not mean that she would, too. She is her own person and I have to support that.

Even to this day, Cher stays in contact with a few friends she made that first year at the public middle school. I couldn't have been happier about a choice we made…together.

"There were times when, in middle school and junior high, I didn't have a lot of friends. But my mom was always my friend. Always." – Taylor Swift

Chapter Objectives…

- ✓ Mothers, it's important to take the time to listen to your daughter, to honestly hear what she is saying, and be willing to compromise with her even if you are very worried about making any big changes.

- ✓ When we work together and compromise, we are able to create lasting memories we'll never forget.

Chapter 7

Learning Life Lessons On Your Own

As much as we try, as mothers, to help our daughters avoid making mistakes, more times than not our children tend to learn life's biggest lessons on their own. Sometimes, they simply learn by doing and seeing for themselves and the results end up pretty okay. Like a child refusing to believe the soup really *is* too hot like mom said, and then gobbling down a spoonful and burning their tongue a little.

Not ideal, but no long-term harm, and next time they'll remember to blow on it, right?

But, other times, they learn the hard way, and their mistakes have longer lasting consequences.

Like one time that Cher got sick of having long hair and decided to give herself some nice layers.

With a butcher's knife.

She only cut a couple of inches off. Unfortunately, those inches were right in the front, and she wound up looking like she got chased by a Weedwacker-wielding psycho who finally caught up to her.

We tried to even it out, but what can you do with a ¼-inch stump of hair smack in the middle of your forehead?

Not much!

It took months to grow it out and, while the consequences weren't dangerous or life-altering, she took a lot of heat from her brothers and other kids at school about it.

As mothers, we want to protect our daughters from those types of mistakes. Heck, we want to protect them from everything, don't we? How many times have you found yourself sitting at the dentist or doctor with your child in the chair, making magical-thought deals with everyone from God to the Tooth Fairy if you could just switch seats with them and take their pain away?

But we can't. And, as bad as it feels, we can't protect them from themselves and their mistakes, either. Nor should we try.

Not all the time.

How will they ever learn about consequences? How will they ever manage in the real world, when you can't be there every day at their jobs or in their marriages, to clean up their messes?

If your daughter remembers they have a project due TOMORROW and you run out to the store and buy construction paper and glue and markers and then stay up all night doing said project on their behalf, you might help them get a good grade that day. But what about in fifteen years, when their boss is waiting on a report they were supposed to provide for a big client the next day? Who's going to bail her out there? Have you robbed her of the ability to stay strong and perform under pressure because you decided to be her own, personal "fixer"?

Have you offset the much needed confidence that would allow her to say, "I know I can buckle down and do that, because I've done it in the past!"

It is one thing to teach and guide our daughters on the difference between right and wrong, but it's another for our daughters to be put into a situation that is going to test their ability to choose the right path and manage the consequences on their own.

That doesn't mean you can't be a great support system for her, though. No matter the mistakes or choices our daughters make in life, it's important for mothers to practice unconditional love. When our daughters do make bad decisions from time to time, they are going to be feeling that guilt and regret. They won't need a judge at that moment, but a guardian angel to help them through the hard times. Be there with the tissues. Hold her when she cries. If she's an adult, commiserate over a glass of wine or a nice meal.

There is no greater gift than your mother or daughter being there for you through life's hardest trials and tribulations. Mothers are like guides who give advice and also give comfort when the wrong path has been chosen (no matter how much we tried to warn them!) The more you are there for each other, the more you can rely on each other when the very worst thing happens.

But never forget that your job as a mother is ultimately to raise a strong, self-reliant, capable woman. So make sure to practice unconditional, but sometimes tough, love. Even when it hurts you both...

Life Experience: Summer Camp, by Cher

Some lessons you have to learn on your own regardless of the advice you've been given before.

When I was fourteen, I went away from home for a summer long sleep-away camp. My parents thought it would be a good idea for me to give it a try. They hoped I would learn some self-reliant skills from being away from home for so long and that I would come home with more confidence and plenty of fun stories to share with the family based on my experiences.

When I went to this sleep-away camp, it was the last year that I could qualify to go, so everyone attending already had their 'cliques' and their own friends because they had attended several years in a row. Luckily, I had a friend to go with me, but Melissa and I were both 'the new girls in town'.

Now, I did end up having a 'camp boyfriend' and we ended up really liking each other and having a good time hanging out with each other while I was there. But one night, towards the end of the camp experience, I met this girl named Jillian. She was from my hometown and I knew her from high school because she was one of the popular girls at my school. Seeing her, I knew I wanted to get in with 'that crowd'. Plus, I wasn't having the best time at camp, despite my camp boyfriend and Melissa.

So when Jillian told me and Melissa that she had some alcohol and asked if we wanted to drink with her and her friends before the camp-wide dance party later that night, we were in!

At the time, I had never had the opportunity to drink much. Though I had taken a few sips here and there at different family events, I had never really consumed enough to get tipsy. Melissa and I both hoped that a few drinks would help us loosen up and make some more friends at camp.

It was all really clandestine and sneaky. Before the dance, we skulked through the woods in the dark. When we got there, Jillian had a full Sprite bottle filled with vodka. Melissa and I split the bottle between us, and together we ended up drinking the whole thing without realizing how that would affect us.

And, man, did it affect us. Especially Melissa. By the time we got to the dance party, she went from being this quiet, shy girl, to twerking and dancing all over the place. One minute, we were sitting on a stump, tearfully promising to be friends forever. The next, we were grabbing each other, screeching, "Oh my gosh, gurl, this is my song!" and then dancing and singing like two fools. I look back on that night today and thank God that "Oops, I Did it Again" didn't start playing. There is no doubt in my mind that, in my drunken state, I would've started belting it out into that empty Sprite bottle, ended on that big closing split, and wound up with a branch up my hoo-ha for my troubles.

As it turned out, no branch extraction was necessary. We *did* get caught, though, when the sleep-away camp po-po busted us a little while later because we literally reeked of alcohol. They gave us a stern talking to that night and then made us sleep in the infirmary in case we had alcohol poisoning. Like all drunk people do, I made a vow to never drink again if only I could get out of this without my parents finding out. And, honestly, once we'd gotten into our cots in the infirmary, I was pretty convinced that was going to be the end of it. They were going to let us sleep it off and everything would be okay in the morning.

Spoiler alert: It wasn't.

Come morning, we were called into the camp's main office. Melissa and I were told that we were getting kicked out of sleep-away camp and had to take the first available flight home. After coming face-to-face with the consequences of my actions, I felt like garbage. Even though I didn't really love camp, all of these emotions started pouring through me. My parents had spent a lot of their hard-earned money to give me this opportunity that not a lot of kids had, and I'd blown it. I also felt bad because, despite Melissa making her own decision, if I hadn't befriended Jillian and finagled us an invite, none of that would've even happened to her. Not to mention that I had a camp boyfriend who I wasn't even going to be able to say good-bye to, along with my other camp friends, and I knew this was my last year to go.

Not the way I wanted to end that experience at all.

"A mother knows what her child's gone through, even if she didn't see it herself." – Pramoedya Ananta Toer

But the very worst part was when they made me sit in the room as they called my mom. The camp director told her that Melissa and I had been caught drinking alcohol on camp grounds and that the camp has a zero tolerance for that.

I could literally hear my mother's shrill, stunned response coming from the receiver even though I was six feet away.

"That can't be right…Are you sure you're talking about *my* Cher?"

My mother, bless her heart, just couldn't believe that the camp was calling about *her* sweet, obedient daughter. I could hear her protesting to the director as the call went on.

"Cher is a really good kid. I can't believe it."

And though the camp director agreed that while, overall, I was a very good camper, the camp still had a zero tolerance for alcohol and he had no choice but to send me home.

I could tell that my mother was completely shocked when the director handed me the phone because all she said to me was to make sure I packed everything and that she and my father would meet me at the airport the next day.

By the time I got off the plane, my hands were shaking and clammy and I felt like I was going to throw up. All I could think about was how disappointed in me they were going to be and how much trouble I was in. I was already upset with my own behavior and for being so selfish. Now I had to face what I'd put them through.

Imagine my surprise when I met my parents at the airport and they just hugged me. They didn't yell. They didn't demand an explanation, even though I'm sure they were upset with my actions. I think that, when they saw my face, they knew that I had disappointed myself as much as I had them, and that this was a lesson I had learned for myself.

My mother explained that she wasn't going to punish me for drinking. I had already lost camp privileges and had to go home humiliated. Plus, I was clearly punishing myself enough already. She made me promise not to do it again, and that was the end of it. According to her, there was no need to beat it, the horse was already dead.

I was so grateful and relieved. The fact was that, at fourteen, I just didn't understand the control needed to not overdo it or any of that important stuff you need to know when you start drinking. Her recognizing that and choosing not to add insult to injury was so beneficial to me. I didn't take advantage of that leniency, or take a mile because she gave me that inch. Instead, it made me want to be that good kid she'd always had faith that I was.

It made me think harder about my choices and their consequences in the future. It also made me realize that she had my back and that she knew me, probably better than anyone else in the world, because she knew that it was a one-time mistake, and really out of my character. This really strengthened our bond and made us that much closer.

Hers was a winning strategy, and one I swore I would implement when I had my own family.

Does that mean I never got in trouble?

I wish!

I still had to keep to my curfew and, when I broke it, there would be a swift punishment from my parents, even if I was only a few minutes late. Despite being a good kid, there were still plenty of times during my growing up stages where I made mistakes and got grounded. But that time, the lesson was already learned, and there was no point in kicking me when I was down.

Now that I'm grown, I know my mother won't always be physically beside me as I move forward in life. But I also know that my mother is only a phone call away. If need be, I can be home with a quick plane ride. No amount of distance will ever make me feel like my mother is truly far from me. It's quite the opposite. I feel her close beside me as I move forward in my adult life, making the best decisions I can based on my experiences and the knowledge my mother has given me.

When I think about how I want to make my mother proud or show her how much I appreciate her raising me, it gives me motivation to succeed and prove to my parents that their love for me truly helped better not only myself, but those I interact with.

I see myself now as an extension of my mother, like the next generation of what she has been able to instill in me as I grew into the woman I am today. I have this desire to make her happy, to show people what Dawn Hubsher's daughter is capable of. I want to express to them the kindness she has always shown me, the care and dedication that seems to be unwavering. Through everything that I do, I know that my mother is with me, and that gives me the strength and confidence to always try and succeed the best way I can.

Even when I don't always do it all perfectly.

Chapter Objectives...

✓ As daughters grow and experience life for themselves to gain their own understanding and wisdom, mothers are like guides who give advice and also give comfort when the wrong path has been chosen, no matter how much we tried to warn them.

✓ Don't knock your daughter down more when she is already at her lowest point.

✓ Sometimes your daughter will learn a life lesson on her own without the need for you to teach her.

Chapter 8

Being Open With Your Mom Or Daughter

When mothers are open and honest with their daughters, it allows their daughter to feel more comfortable opening up to her mother in return.

Mothers have experienced a lot of what their daughters are going through, from changes to their bodies and what it means to become a woman, to learning how to protect themselves and treat their bodies with respect. By keeping the lines of communication open and not freaking out when these things come up, it gives a daughter the confidence to be open. This allows things that might seem scary or daunting to be accepted more easily or even celebrated.

A daughter's first menstrual period can be a cherished experience with her mother instead of one that the daughter has to be terrified or nervous about because she doesn't truly understand what is going on with her body and she doesn't feel comfortable talking to her mother about it.

A first kiss can stir up all sorts of crazy emotions and

hormones, but if she can talk to her mom about it, she can get help processing those feelings and understand that it isn't shameful or weird. It's normal.

Then there are those times that every mother dreads. There are countless things in this world we don't want our daughters to experience or even think of trying. We can choose to bury our heads in the sand and pretend that our daughter "would never!" or we can accept that kids push boundaries, test limits, and make mistakes. That's how they learn. The best we can do is to educate them on the reality of things that they are likely to experience or consider experiencing and give it to them straight.

If not, we're leaving Google and friends their own age to fill in the blanks. Need we remind you that there are kids who still think babies come from storks in this day and age? And if a pre-teen Googles how to get pregnant, they might find a great, informative article, or they might find some fetish porn flick featuring gangbangs with pregnant women.

Not ideal.

But what if our daughter wants to *try* this thing, as well? Maybe they want gauges instead of traditional earrings. Or a tattoo. It can be as simple as our daughter wanting to try alcohol for the first time. Regardless of what your daughter comes to you wanting to try or experience, it's important not to let emotions take over. Shutting her down will only ensure that, the next time she wants to try something, she just won't tell you about it. Instead, listen carefully and thoroughly discuss the pros and cons and potential ramifications of her choice and hope she makes the right one.

When the shoe is on the other foot, it's also important for daughters to step up to the plate and hear some things she might not want to hear, as well. Maybe your mother is experiencing menopause, or wants you to hold her hand at what might be a scary mammogram. There are plenty of instances in a woman's life where we want a best friend with us to help us through the experience. Don't let embarrassment or silly social conventions keep you from being open, because no one is better suited for the job than your mother or daughter.

Life Experience: Our Love Is Our Drug, by Cher

I remember a time when I came home from a sleep-away camp (not the one that I had been kicked out of, because I'm pretty sure that one had my face emblazoned on a Most Wanted-style poster with the word "BANNED" underneath). This one was around the time I was going into 9th grade, and I had this urge to try a cigarette. A lot of my friends, even though we were all very young, had smoked cigarettes and had talked about how they'd tried it. It wasn't that I wanted to become a smoker, I just wanted to see what all the talk was about.

My mother had told me that she had never smoked before, either, and that kind of made me feel guilty for wanting to try one, but I did it anyway.

I wasn't alone, though.

Instead of just sneaking off, I was honest and told my mother how I was feeling. We went through the whole discussion, pros and cons, and about how bad it was for a person's health. We agreed that becoming a smoker was not something I would ever do, but I still wanted to try it, one time.

My mother's reply?

"If you're going to try it, I'm going to try it, too."

I asked if we could do it at the same time, and she agreed. Not because she wanted me to smoke a cigarette. But because she *knew* I was going to, with or without her. Wouldn't it be better if we did it together than for me to lie to her about it and smoke with someone else who might not have my best interest at heart or might peer pressure me into doing it again?

Since I had told my mother what I had planned to do, she chose to actually listen to what I had to say and see what she could do to help remove my curiosity in the safest, most controlled manner possible. She also later confided in me that she hoped to drop a few more hints about how unhealthy it was in the process.

At our house, we had a cute little ashtray with a few cigarettes in it for people to use when they were visiting the house. It was more of a courtesy than an outwards expression that my parents smoked. That day, we went to the little ashtray and took a cigarette to light.

"If we're going to do this, we might as well do it right," my mom said with a shrug.

She bustled out of the room and I followed her, totally confused, until she stopped at her bedroom closet and pulled out a cropped, leather jacket.

"Get yours. If I'm going to smoke, I'm going to look cool, like The Fonz when I do it."

I ran to my room and grabbed my own leather jacket and, together, we headed out to the back stoop and lit up.

Needless to say, as we both took our first inhale, looking "cool" left the building. We both instantly started hacking and coughing and tearing up. But through it all, we were laughing our "butts" off.

We quickly learned that cigarette smoking wasn't for us. Still, we will always look back on that experience of how it was fun trying it together, both of us for the first time, realizing together that we didn't need cigarettes in our lives. We could simply enjoy each other's company instead.

Love is our drug.

So, how do you create a relationship with your mother or daughter where you feel comfortable talking about anything and everything?

Be open. Share details about your personal life, your fears and hopes for the future. Do you honestly love your job or are you just doing it to pay the bills? Are you feeling fulfilled?

Talk to your mother or daughter about these things. Be open and honest about the bits and pieces deep down inside. By getting in the habit of sharing the most intimate parts of yourself, you'll then be more comfortable talking about the bigger things in life.

The basic principle is taking action that is genuine and authentic.

Don't overthink it. Just do it.

A Limitless Mother-Daughter Relationship

If you want to have this type of close relationship with your daughter, too, you have to be willing to be real with her. There is no point putting on a show and limiting conversation topics. Be real and authentic with her no matter how old or young she is. You want this bond with your mother or daughter to grow stronger so, if possible, it needs to start early on. If you are just now trying to mend a broken relationship or perhaps you are becoming a mother to an adoptive older daughter, all you have to do is try *now*, even if the bond hasn't been nurtured from a young age.. Some topics might be awkward to discuss, and sometimes your daughter will come to you quite unexpectedly. The best method to tackle difficult or awkward topics of conversation is to be respectful to each other and be dedicated to truly listening and understanding.

Regardless of the advice mothers might give their daughters when it comes to serious life situations like sex, a daughter still has her own free agency to choose what to do with the information she has been given by her mother. So, mothers, remember to practice unconditional love. Our daughters might not do the things we would ideally like them to do, or not to do, but we must continue to love and respect them, no matter what.

"One of the most important relationships we have is the relationship we have with our mothers."
— Iyanla Vanzant

Chapter Objectives...

✓ When a mother is very open and honest with her daughter about things in life that she will need to eventually know, then her daughter will feel more comfortable talking to her mother when those life situations do happen.

✓ Regardless of what your daughter comes to you wanting to try or experience, it's important not to let emotions take over your initial response.

✓ By getting in the habit of sharing the most intimate parts of yourself, you'll then be more comfortable talking about the bigger things in life that need to be discussed between a mother and daughter.

✓ It is better to prepare a daughter for the real world than pretend like it doesn't exist.

Chapter 9

Working Together

Having shared goals is an amazing way of strengthening the bond in any relationship. This holds true for mothers and daughters, as well. Not only does it foster more communication and conversation, it also gives you a reason to spend time together. For some people, that might mean something long-term, like having a little side-hustle business that you create together. For others, it might mean something less involved, like planning a favorite aunt's surpise retirement party. And for others still, it might be a plot to get your father/husband to start eating right and taking better care of his health.

Whatever the goal or task at hand, when a mother and daughter put their heads (and hearts) together, they can manifest and create all sorts of amazing things. Despite being in different fields of work and oftentimes living in different parts of the country, we have managed to work together many, many times. Each experience resulted in our becoming even closer and improving our communication skills with one another. And, even more rewarding was each of us getting to see the other show their strengths and talents and truly shine.

Try to find some common thread of interest, whether it be a favorite charity to coordinate an event for or planning an extended family getaway, and do the work together. We think you'll find it just as rewarding as we do!

Life Experience: My Super Sweet 16, by Cher

Growing up, I would always watch this show called *My Super Sweet 16* on MTV. I would watch the show thinking these sweet sixteen birthday parties were just amazing.

At one point, I even thought I would love to be on the show. Since I was already planning a sweet sixteen party of my own, I started to become obsessed with the thought. After hemming and hawing about it, I finally decided to apply. I knew that it would be a long shot, but I wanted to at least try.

I went online and filled out the application and sent it off with a wish and a prayer.

To my surprise, a few weeks later, I got a phone call from MTV. They had loved my application and wanted to see more! Now that this was actually real instead of just a pipedream, it was time to talk to my mom about it.

I was nervous at first, and rightfully so. She gave me a flat-out no. She was afraid that having me on TV at such a young age would potentially make me a target for bullies, but also that creeps and perverts might see me and do something crazy.

I already knew that I wanted to do something in communications and in the public eye, so I sat down and made a really well thought out list of pros and cons and presented it to her.

Pro: Getting a much-desired jump-off in the entertainment industry.

Con: Potentially catching the eye of some creeper, getting kidnapped and tied to a radiator for the rest of my life.

To me, it was a no brainer. To her, not so much.

But after a long discussion with her and my dad, they agreed to let me try, as it was a long shot, but if I got it they knew that they would be helping to make my dream a reality.

In order to move on to the next step, MTV wanted to see me interact on camera and what my personality was like. I ended up borrowing my father's video camera and I had my mother record me basically being silly and having fun.

After recording the video, I sent a copy through the mail, as instructed. Just putting it in the mailbox was a thrill!

I got a call from MTV a few weeks later and they wanted to hear more about what I was planning for my sweet sixteen party! They even took the time to talk to my mom, as well, which really helped settle her nerves about the whole thing. They also explained to her what they looked for in the ultimate sweet sixteen party. We had already been planning a pretty amazing bash, but we had to meet certain criteria to make it onto the show. By that point, my mom knew how much I wanted this opportunity, and she decided to do everything she could to help me secure it.

Only, MTV ended up wanting to speak with our party planner. Now, anyone who knows the Hubshers knows that we throw big, fun parties. But we've always been our own party planners with the help of our good friend, Andrea Szmiga. We would get these great ideas and she would always help us make them a reality, creating these wonderful experiences together.

INCOMING TEA ALERT:

drops voice to a whisper

Unwilling to let the dream die, my amazing mom ended up changing her voice and acting like the party planner, since at this point we had not even discussed the party with Andrea.

It was hilarious but we had to keep it together as she chattered away in this fake accent that sounded like the heroine in a 1950's movie. We both knew we needed to get over this obstacle if the show was going to happen. There were several back and forth phone interviews over the course of several weeks that kept us both on our toes.

But, finally, we got the call! MTV wanted us on the show! They were going to start filming the day I got home from the trip I was on. I was so excited, I called my mom to tell her the good news and that I couldn't believe this was actually happening now. It was such a dream come true!

The moment I walked off the plane, video cameras were there filming every minute. We went home in a limo and began filming the show immediately. The film crew stayed for three weeks and filmed us. Even though viewers only saw 30 minutes of the craziest moments of those three weeks, the camera crew had been filming what felt like 24/7. Luckily, my mom realized that her concerns were a result of her being overprotective and she was able to fully enjoy the process without thinking I was going to get serial murdered.

It turned into such a wonderful and fun experience that I got to share with her. Together, we planned every minute of the party, from how I was going to deliver my invitations, to what dress I would wear. We decided on a magic act for my grand arrival where I was able to be the assistant, and it was fun to learn the ins and outs of magic. Not only was the planning of the party such a fun experience with my mom, it was another building block in our relationship.

Through our willingness (and genuine desire!) to work together, and our ability to compromise we were able to create lasting memories we'll never forget.

"Mothers and daughters together are a powerful force to be reckoned with." — Melia Keeton-Digby

Chapter Objectives...

- ✓ Working together toward shared goals can bring a mother and daughter closer.

- ✓ The impossible is almost always possible.

- ✓ Never underestimate what you are capable of.

- ✓ Working together can help you achieve great things.

Chapter 10

Trust and Reliability

"All I want is for my children to have more than I had, go further than I ever did, and be happier than imaginable."- Dawn Hubsher

Being Reliable

As daughters, ideally, we grow up knowing our mothers will always be there for us. No matter what we do, no matter the mistakes or the choices we will make, the one person we can always call in the middle of the night that will be there for us is our mother.

But did you know that as daughters we can do the same for our mothers? It's easy to think that they can handle anything, do anything, and come out stronger than ever. But every woman, at some point in their life, mother or not, will have a day where something happens and she just can't muster the strength to put her cape on and be Super Woman for everyone. One of those rock bottom times where life tests her and she hits her breaking point.

Whether it's a divorce or perhaps the death of a spouse or loved one, there will be a time when your mother will need her daughter just as much as you have needed her your entire life.

It's in those times that we see the importance of true reliability. I mean that ride or die kind of mentality that makes you drop everything.

And I mean, everything.

From that hair appointment with that fancy new stylist you had to book six months in advance to a hot date for your very first wedding anniversary. From missing an important meeting at work to passing on a lucrative side-hustle job so that you can get to the airport, pay that ludicrous same day airfare, and be by your mother's side.

The same holds true on the other side of the coin. When life takes a turn for the worst, it's often unexpected. Maybe your daughter's fiancé was busted sexting the hostess at their favorite restaurant. Or maybe she missed out on that big promotion that she was sure she was getting and worked so hard for. Showing your dedication for your mother or daughter during this time will help ease the pain.

Does this mean that the next time your mom messages you with a 911 telling you that she forgot to DVR The Bachelor that you need to leave work and DVR it for her?

Of course not. That doesn't qualify as a crisis (even though it might feel like one!)

But you know her. You can hear it in her voice. The one

that sounds a hair away from breaking. The one that, out loud, might be saying words like, "It's okay. I'll be fine," but under it all, is really saying, "I'm having a really hard time and I need you right now." Don't second guess your gut instinct on that. If she needs you, do everything in your power to be there so she knows she can count on you in her time of need. Then, lift her up in her times of sorrow. Comfort her when her heart is breaking or burdened. Be willing to share that burden with your mother, to help her through trials in life, and remind her that she is doing a great job at being *your* mother.

And when things are good again, keep that same mentality. Ensure that you're reliable even when the other person isn't necessarily in need. There might be a time when you are so busy in your day that when you see a phone call coming in from your mother or daughter that you might ignore it, knowing you simply can't dedicate one extra minute to something else when you're already focused on so many other things. But make sure you call back, no matter how busy you get. And when you can answer? Do. Be available to take their phone calls, to have them over to the house, to plan specific times each week or month to just be with them. This not only shows that you love them and want them in your life, but it also expresses that you are there for them, rain *or* shine. It is one thing to love them, but it's another to let them see your dedication through authentic action.

Whether you talk to your mother or daughter every few days, every Sunday night on the dot, or every evening with a simple text, the point is to keep the lines of communication open and strong.

Daughters, you might not know it, but you will be your mother's lifeline at one point or another. Mothers, you keep working hard at being the greatest mother *you* can be. And know that, come what may, you always have one another to count on.

"The first lesson every child of Athena learned: Mom was the best at everything, and you should never, ever suggest otherwise." – Rick Riordan

Life Experience: A Mother in Need, by Dawn

It's a situation no mother ever wants to have to face. The time that you're forced to take a backseat and let your daughter take the wheel. The time you have no choice but to lean on her, and, in the worst of times, lean **hard.**

We always want to be strong and handle our trauma and pain ourselves so as not to burden those we love, but sometimes life gives you more than you can handle on your own.

This was the case for me when Cher was in her later teen years and I began to have very acute bouts of a disease called Ulcerative Colitis. I won't darken your day with the gory details, but suffice it to say that a flare up meant, regardless of where we were or what we were doing, if I had to go?

I had to *go.*

It was painful. It was humiliating. It made me feel weak and terrible. But through it all, Cher was there. My little rock of support and a fountain of excellent excuses to manage my sudden disappearances.

Without me ever asking, if we were at a party and I was gone too long, she was armed and ready.

"Oh, my mom. She's a fancy soap aficionado. Probably in there pawing through all of the different scents, I bet she's in heaven right now!"

Or, *"Sorry, my mom had to step away for an important call. She said she'd be back as soon as she can."*

This disease brought other fun treats along with it, as well. There were days that I would get dressed up only to look in the mirror and find that my stomach was so bloated, I looked five months pregnant. How do I know that this wasn't just me being paranoid? Because one time we were shopping and a "helpful stranger" stopped and asked how far along I was.

But there was Cher again, and instead of laughing at what might've seemed funny from the outside looking in, she instantly tried to comfort me, insisting it must have just been the way I was standing. She even went through a three-minute demo of slouching and standing and slumping and straightening and telling me how posture could make anyone look like they have a bun in the oven, even her with her tiny frame!

She didn't take a breath before continuing on to tell me how proud I should be that people still thought I looked young enough to be pregnant.

But Cher was more than just my confidence booster. She was also always the one who kept track of my doctor appointments and made sure I got where I needed to go.

During my colonoscopies they would have to put me under anesthesia and when I would come out of it, I would always have to pee. Instead of letting the nurse help, Cher always stepped up, knowing I was more comfortable with her. She would help me in the bathroom, change my clothes and do anything she could to make the process more bearable. And what made it even better? She was always happy to do it.

She also helped manage my care even when I wasn't having a flare up, making sure I didn't cancel doctor appointments and even coming with me to take notes and make sure I was eating what I was supposed to and taking my meds.

Cher's commitment to my health at such a young age during those difficult times brings tears to my eyes, because not only was she empathetic, but it also showed me that she saw me as a human being and a woman aside from just being her mother.

I've never been more proud, and I've never felt more supported in my life. Knowing you can count on someone is a priceless gift. In a mother-daughter relationship, be ready to give it *and* receive it.

But reliability isn't just about being there when someone you love needs you. It's also about earning and giving trust, and being truthful with one another. But with headstrong teenagers, that's not always going to happen...

Life Experience: Lies, by Cher

I would've ranked the whole drinking at camp thing as my worst transgression in high school, but it was another bad choice entirely that takes the number one spot, and it's one that pains me to this day.

During my senior year in high school, I asked my mom if I could stay the night at a friend's house. My mother has always been leery of me staying the night at a girlfriend's because she would be worried about the other people that would be staying or that something bad would happen to me. Often, I had friends sleep over at my house instead of the other way around. But when I asked her this particular time, she allowed it because she knew the friend and her family very well. She also knew that college wasn't far off, and she might as well get used to me being away.

While I didn't lie about the fact that I was staying the night with my friend, I neglected to mention that we were staying at her parents' timeshare condo with a few other people…none of whom were her parents.

Included in the list of others was the guy I was dating at the time.

Truth be told, it wasn't exactly a wild night. As a group, we had fun talking and eating pizza. A few people had a couple of drinks, but even that was tame, and most were either just dancing or hanging out.

In the morning, we went back to my friend's actual house where my mom picked me up. I told her that I had had a great time with my friend, and because we share so much with one another, I started to talk freely. I mentioned that I forgot my hair straightener and when she suggested she turn around so we could pick it up, I froze.

Quick heads up: I'm a terrible liar. But more than that, my mom has a BS radar like you wouldn't believe and she knows me better than anyone. Instantly, she stopped the car and turned to face me.

"Cher, I know you're lying. Just tell me what really happened. Where were you last night?"

In a panic, I tried to keep up the ruse, but I couldn't do it and wound up spilling the whole story. Piece by piece, I told more and more of the truth until she discovered who was all really there at my friend's parents' condo.

My mother was pretty upset that I had basically spent the night with my boyfriend, even though everyone was sleeping in the same room. The fact that she didn't really like him made it even worse.

She was usually so loving and sweet to me, but it was like a switch had been flipped inside her. Completely upset, the second we got home, she called my friend and told her that she was going to call her parents. She spent the next twenty minutes essentially tag-team screaming at us both, back and forth.

It wasn't fun.

But what was a thousand times worse was when she hung up the phone and tears filled her eyes.

I've already told you how strong my mom is, and I can't think of anything that hurts me more than to see her cry, so I was gutted by this.

"Mom, I swear, nothing happened!" I told her, begging her to stop crying.

But she swiped the tears from her face and let out a harsh laugh. "You think I'm mad that you slept somewhere you weren't supposed to? No! What hurts most is that you lied to me about it. I thought our relationship was…different. You didn't trust me enough to tell me the truth."

It hadn't occurred to me at the time, but, in her mind, me lying was breaking the special bond that we'd always had. No matter what, we should be able to tell each other anything, even if we don't like the response. The whole point of being honest, even with our mistakes, is the ability to work out a solution together. The fact that I so cavalierly betrayed that unspoken promise completely devastated her.

The reason I had lied in the first place is because I knew my mother wouldn't have allowed me to go if she knew the truth. I really wanted to have this experience of staying the night with just my friends, no adults around, to create special moments that I would never forget. I justified my actions because I felt that I deserved to have normal teenage experiences of staying up all night just hanging out, away from the outside world.

"If you tell the truth, you don't have to remember anything." – Mark Twain

Now that I think about the whole situation, though, I realize that if I had told her my reasons, she actually might have let me go. Sure, I'd have had to make some compromises. My boyfriend would've been off the guest list, and she might have insisted that my friend's mom was on board. But I'm confident we could have come up with a compromise. Instead, I robbed her of the opportunity to show her level of trust in me and I hurt our relationship.

As I watched my mother continue to be upset for days afterwards, I really learned the lesson that there is nothing worth lying over if this is the pain it would cause.

This taught me that lies will get you into more trouble than just telling the truth. I believe you always need to express your feelings and always speak from your heart. Because my mother and I have such a long and strong bond, she forgave me more quickly than she probably should have, and I was able to earn back her trust, but I never forgot the look on her face…like I'd kicked her right in the gut.

And I have done my darnedest since then to make sure I'd never see it again.

But what about "white lies"?

This is a question we get a lot! "Dawn, Cher, you say you always tell each other the truth! What if one of you gets a bad haircut, or buys a really unfortunate dress that makes your butt look saggy and it's too late to change it? You're going to tell the truth then, too?"

As hard as it is to believe, the answer is yes.

Sometimes we are quick to feel like a lie is needed to prevent someone from getting hurt. We justify hiding the truth from our loved one, thinking it will benefit them in the short-term. Other times we lie because we want to be able to do something even though we know our mother or daughter would not approve. It's hard finding a balance between what we want to do and what we know is right. Oftentimes we choose what feels good over what we know is the right choice. No matter what justifications we use to lie, though, there is a price tag that comes along with it. Either the liar pays by feeling guilty or getting caught and losing trust, or the person being lied to pays because they don't realize they look like a sack of cottage cheese in that dress and they wind up wearing it again and bumping into their ex.

Does anyone want to hear that the outfit they're wearing isn't flattering? Not really. But part of being there for someone and building unshakable trust is telling it like it is. On the other side of that equation, as the person receiving that uncomfortable truth, accept it in the manner it is being offered; with love, great care, and the desire for what is best for that person. So long as your intentions come from love and a good place, the truth will indeed set you free.

And it will also make your mother-daughter relationship that much stronger.

"Mothers, look after your daughters, keep them near you, keep their confidence — that they may be true and faithful." — Elmina S. Taylor

Chapter Objectives...

✓ Truly "being there" for your mother or daughter means doing it reliably.

✓ For daughters, as you grow older and gain life experience, you'll need that knowledge one day to help your mother, as well.

✓ Reliability is about being able to count on someone to not only be there for you, but to also tell you the truth.

✓ When you go to your mother or daughter with the truth, remind them that you don't want to lie to them even though what you're saying might hurt sometimes.

Chapter 11

Finding Independence

There will come a time in every mother's life when she will have to send her baby girl off into the world. The years go by in a blink and then you're taking your daughter to college or helping her pack before she moves out of the house into her first apartment.

Eventually, every mother has to let her daughter go in some way or another. Regardless of the distance between a mother and daughter, there are still plenty of ways to stay connected. With this knowledge, mothers should take the time to prepare daughters to stand on their own two feet and face the world. It will be up to the daughter to use everything they've learned from home to create their independence.

Some mothers might be resistant to letting their daughters go, and try to hang on with all their might. They might become overbearing, constantly wanting to check in and not giving their child some personal space in which to grow. This is a strategy that can backfire and might push them farther away. Trust me, I have been there! It can be tough, but there is a way to find a balance that both of you are comfortable with. For some people, that might mean weekly check-ins or Sunday dinners. For others (like us! lol) that might mean daily chats and matching outfits, even when we're not living in the same state! There are plenty of ways to allow your daughter her freedom and independence while still remaining an important part of her life, whether it be a care package from you every once in a while simply reminding her how much you love her, or even just a quick text.

The point is, you have to remember that you've prepared your daughter for the real world. You've taught her to treat others with kindness, to cook, to balance a checkbook, and how to change a spare tire on her own car. You've taught her all the things she will need to be a self-reliant, law-abiding citizen. Now you've got to step back a little, and let her take the world by storm!

Again, the key here? Is balance…

Life Experience: Exiled To Independence, by Cher

After My Super Sweet Sixteen birthday party aired, my mother and I got a lot of really good feedback. The episode received a very high viewer rating, and MTV called us back to do another show. This time, though, I was largely kept in the dark about the process because this show was called Exiled. The basic premise was that MTV would take the sweet sixteeners from the previous series from our cushy lives and put each one of us into a totally different (and very challenging) environment.

And, we would only be informed of our destinations once the show started taping.

Needless to say, my mother was both nervous and hesitant, being the type of mom that doesn't even like the idea of me spending the night over at a friend's house. But she knew I'd be in good hands with the MTV production team and figured it would be a great experience, so she agreed. She also knew it would be a great introduction to a little more independence since I would soon be going off to college.

So, with the cameras rolling, I came home one day from school and was told by my mother that MTV had agreed to have me on their new show where I was going to be exiled…to the jungles of Panama. I had time to pack, and the next morning, I was on a plane.

As terrifying as it sounds, underneath the nerves, I was actually very excited. I knew that I wouldn't be made to do anything that would get me seriously injured, so I knew I could go into this experience with an open mind and simply try my best. Looking back, it wound up being one of the most amazing experiences of my life.

I was sent across the world to Panama to live with a local native tribe, doing all the things they needed to do every day to survive. I had to sleep on a hard-wooden floor with nails poking up through the wood with only a small covering between me and the floor. I had to sleep with a mosquito netting around me to protect me from mosquito-borne illnesses. I had to cook all of my meals over a fire and collect plantains from trees to eat. I even tried spear fishing (although I purposely missed because I couldn't stand the thought of killing the fish).

I'm not going to lie. It was hard and lonely and uncomfortable at points, but it was also extremely humbling and I was amazed by the people I met and their culture. It gave me a whole new perspective on my own life, and I learned more about people and humanity than I had at any other point growing up. To date, it was one of the most wonderful and rewarding experiences I've ever had and it also did exactly what my mother hoped it would. It made me learn that I could be away from home and use the lessons my mother taught me. To be kind, respectful, and work hard. I couldn't think of a better way to prepare myself for leaving my home because it gave me the confidence I would need to be successful at college.

After all, what was going to be so hard about sleeping in a dorm and eating ramen noodles? At least I had a bed and food to eat! It made me feel a lot of gratitude for the things that I had, and I'll never forget it.

"Being a mother is an attitude, not a biological relation."
– Robert A. Heinlein

During my time in Panama, I wasn't able to speak to my mother at all. I knew that had to have been really hard for her because she couldn't talk to me to see how I was doing. She had to rely on the producers to give her updates. This was a good practice run for her, as well, because soon we'd be separated for long periods of time.

When I started my first week of college shortly after this

experience, I actually arrived at my first class covered in henna tattoos that the native tribe had bestowed upon me as a parting gift. It was a great ice-breaker and helped me make friends quickly, as other students noticed my tattoos and wanted to know how or why I got them.

The experience in Panama also made me realize that I could trust myself to make decisions on my own, using my head and my heart to lead me. But, as my mother often says, "I am a mother and a mother is for life, and I will always be there to guide my children." What a blessing, because even then, as I was growing into a woman, I still needed my mom...just in a different way.

It was time for her to bite the bullet and do what she did when I was learning to walk;

Stand back, hold her breath, and let me stand on my own two feet, even if I stumbled sometimes.

Spoiler alert: She aced it.

A Love That Knows No Distance

Regardless of the physical distance between a mother or daughter, it doesn't have to equate to an emotional or mental distance between them. With modern technology, it's super easy to stay connected. A simple text or phone call is all that is needed to re-affirm the mother-daughter bond. Showing love to one another is as simple as sending a heart emoji or sending our mother or daughter a package in the mail after a few clicks on Amazon. If you make the effort to keep that bond alive and strong when you're apart, when you *do* get to spend time together again face to face, it will be like no time passed at all...

"My mom is literally a part of me. You can't say that about many people except relatives, and organ donors."
— Carrie Latet

Life Experience: Here I Come, by Dawn

When Cher moved to college, I was a wreck. Having her out in the jungle of Panama was bad.

Having her in college three hours away without producers and a film crew in place to keep an eye on her?

Was excruciating.

It took all I had not to try to press her to choose someplace closer to home (or lock her in the attic and keep her there until I was truly ready to let her go). But I did it. I swallowed my fear, bit my lip, and tried not to let her see the tears as she packed her bags.

She must've known. She was so intuitive and empathetic, and we had such a close bond, I shouldn't have been surprised at all when she went out of her way to call me that first night and tell me she was safe and getting ready for bed.

One night turned into two and soon, it became a treasured nightly ritual. A phone call or text, whether it morphed into a 20 minutes-long gab session or just consisted of a quick sentence, to let me know she was home and to say goodnight. She never missed it.

Until she did.

I remember it like it was yesterday. Probably because it was one of the longest and most harrowing nights of my entire life. Cher was in her third year of college, and I knew that she was going out. But I also knew that, no matter what time she got home, I'd get a quick text. Even if I didn't see it before bed, when I would wake up in the middle of the night and look at my phone, there it was. Like a warm hug, easing that anxiety gripping my heart.

So, when the one night came that I didn't get a text from her for the first time in three years (something that we still do to this very day!) I simply couldn't process it. The instant feeling of dread came over me because, deep down inside, I just knew that something wasn't quite right.

It was two in the morning when I finally started calling her, only to get no answer. When that didn't work, I texted her, asking her to just text me back so I at least knew that she was okay.

Still no response, and that's when panic set in.

By that point, she was living off-campus and in an apartment with her brother, but he was out of town for the weekend. There was a guy who lived in the apartment below Cher's who was a bit of an oddball. He always had a lot of people coming in and out of his place and had that spaced out look of a chronic drug user. As my mind continued to race over what could possibly have happened to Cher, four o'clock in the morning came and went and I was suddenly (and, in hindsight, irrationally) certain he had done something to her.

Unable to stand it another second and still unable to get through to her, I woke my husband and told him that I was leaving. I had to drive up to Cher's school to make sure that she was okay. That three hour drive felt like an eternity as every single episode of Dateline ran through my mind.

What if she was in a ditch somewhere?

What if someone had kidnapped her?

The what ifs were driving me insane, but I knew I had to keep it together and drive, pedal to the metal, because the first 48 hours were the most critical if, indeed, something horrible had happened to her.

In hindsight, I realize I could've caused an accident myself, but by that point, I was beyond reason and I couldn't get there fast enough. A part of me was actually hoping a police officer would pull me over so I could tell them what was happening and offer me an escort.

I got there in two hours flat, my bladder so full it felt like it was bursting, and my hands icy-cold and trembling in fear of what I might find. I didn't even turn the car off. I just shoved the door open and ran up the apartment stairs, shouting her name over and over. I got to her door and started banging on it like a madwoman.

And when she opened it a minute later, bleary-eyed and tousled, my knees went weak.

"What's the matter? Is everything okay?"

I nearly fell to the floor in relief. But just as quickly, the fury came right behind it. I'd just spent the entire ride up praying that she would be all right, and now I wanted to kill her myself!

"How could you do that to me? I was terrified!"

I told her what I'd been doing for the past five hours and she felt horrible and instantly began to apologize, explaining that she had dozed off watching TV when she got home without even realizing and her phone was still on silent because she'd turned it down at the movie theater earlier.

Once the adrenaline began to fade, so did my anger, and I hugged her so tight, I almost cracked a rib. Cher felt so bad, she even wound up taking the day off school and playing hooky for a "girls day" like we used to when she was younger. By the time the day was over, I was back to my normal, more rational self and I realized that not everything is an emergency. Sometimes things happen.

But I also have to be honest and own the fact that, no matter how old she is, she will always be my baby girl. And if my instincts called me to make that drive again, I'd do it in a heartbeat. See, being a mother isn't about being perfect. It's about doing the best you can and trying to get it right.

But if loving Cher to the point that I would slay a dragon (or a creepy neighbor) for her is wrong?

Then I don't want to be right.

"No daughter and mother ever live apart, no matter what the distance between them." – Christie Watson

Chapter Objectives...

- ✓ Don't hold your daughter back from testing her independence before leaving home, and don't stand in her way of leaving.

- ✓ Keeping her involved in your life is key to keeping the mother-daughter bond strong even when distance is a variable.

- ✓ A mother's duty does not end when her daughter turns eighteen.

- ✓ You have to listen to your gut because if God forbid something did happen, you would always regret not having gone just to make sure.

Chapter 12

Gratitude

⚜

There is a lot of truth in the old saying, "The best attitude is an attitude of gratitude."

When we speak and act with a grateful heart, we are quicker to give thanks for all the amazing things and people in our lives.

As mothers and daughters, we often express our love for one another, even if it's just a quick little shout-out right before we hang up the phone out of habit. But mothers, how often do we express thanks to our daughters? And daughters, when was the last time you told your mother, "thank you," for being there and for all she's brought to your life? Often, we will call our mothers to tell them we love them and are thinking of them, but do we ever call just to thank them (besides when they've sent us something in the mail)?

Take a moment to reflect on all the different aspects of the relationship you have with your mother or daughter that you can be thankful for — that lifelong friend we can always rely on and call at a moment's notice when we need help. That person who will give you unconditional love when you need it most. That in and of itself is reason enough to be thankful!

So many have lost their mothers or daughters, even just the fact that they are alive and breathing can be looked on with gratitude. The next logical step is to express that gratitude so that your loved one can feel it, too.

It might seem corny, but the next time you speak with your mother or daughter, take the time to tell her thank you. It can be for something little, like remembering to ask how your day has been even though she called to talk about a struggle she's currently having.

"I know you're going through a bad time, and I'm so grateful to have a daughter who, even when she's suffering, is kind and caring enough to ask how I'm doing, too! That's a real blessing to me."

What is the worst thing that can happen?

…Honestly, there is literally zero downside here. No matter how bad her day is going, while it won't solve her problems, she will still feel a warm glow inside from those words, and it cost you nothing to offer them. It's what we over at Dawn-n-Chertown call "a win-win".

Maybe you want to make a bigger statement. Talk about something you've felt for a while but never said out loud, like how grateful you are that she was caring and loving even when perhaps you didn't deserve it, or during a difficult time, when she didn't agree with the choices you made.

A whole book could be written on the things we could take the time to thank our mothers or daughters for, but big or small, the key is to make sure to express our gratitude through words and actions so our loved one knows how thankful we are to have them in our lives.

After all, our mother is the only mother we'll ever have, and our daughter is a gift given to us and us alone. Cherishing it is our duty.

Life Experience: A Little Goes A Long Way, by Dawn

A mother-daughter relationship is not always perfect. If I tried to say that it was, I would be lying to you. There were plenty of times in the past where Cher and I have verbally unloaded on one another. We are human, after all, and will make mistakes from time to time. But we both know deep down that we have each other's best interests at heart and that is what counts most.

How do we know? Because we try to show each other every day.

We all have love for our family members, but *feeling* love and *showing* love are two very different things. And it's the showing that truly counts.

For example, Cher knows in the deepest part of her soul that I will always make time for her no matter what else is happening in my life. This, in turn, allows her to feel surefooted in times of crisis and strong even when she's afraid, because she knows without a shadow of a doubt there is always someone in her corner.

How does she know that?

Because I show her in hundreds of little ways. As a mother, you don't have to buy your daughter diamonds or have her name tattooed on your forehead in some grand display of affection. Constant little reminders that you are there for her and value your relationship are all it takes to build a rock-solid bond.

For example, every once in a while, Cher would be assigned a travel nursing assignment forty minutes from my office. Even though she would only get a thirty-minute lunch break, every time Cher was at that hospital working, I would specifically schedule my workday around her lunch break. I'd skip my coffee breaks and save up that precious time to drive forty minutes to bring over her favorite Starbucks coffee and sit with her while we ate lunch in my car.

Did I have to do it? Of course not. But it was such a bright spot in both of our days and was a small enough sacrifice to have that time with her. Every time she received that travel assignment, I was so excited because I knew I'd have something to look forward to each day she was in town. I also knew it meant so much to her that I would drive the forty minutes there and back just to sit with her for a thirty-minute lunch.

Those silly little lunches full of laughter and chats about our workdays are some of our fondest memories. More importantly, though, they build on our foundation and make it stronger so that when those bad days come, where one of us does or says something we regret, we have so much love and good will saved up in our "banks" that we are able to get through those times much more easily.

"A daughter is a mother's gender partner, her closest ally in the family confederacy, an extension of herself. And mothers are their daughters' role model, their biological and emotional road map, the arbiter of all their relationships." – Victoria Secunda

Life Experience: Being A Mom Doesn't Have To Be A Thankless Job, by Cher

I've been a daughter a long time now, but it's only as I got older that I realized exactly how much my mom did for me.

Right from the get-go, it's basically non-stop, isn't it? In the womb, they give us their very life force to help us grow. Every meal is a shared one. They give up their waistline and their muscle tone to house us and keep us safe. They give up sleep, and going out, and for some mothers, their careers. Not to mention any expectation of privacy and the ability to sneeze without peeing a little.

But it doesn't stop there! They have to give us bottles, and bathe us, and burp us, and comfort us. They have to pick up our toys, and mash our peas, and kiss our booboos. They have to help build our confidence by telling us we are wonderful, even when that's not always the case. It's important to recognize that sacrifice and remember that moms are people, too. They have good days and bad days. Happy times, and sad times. But there are no days off or paid vacations. They are moms every day, starting from the day you come into their lives. And while they have a lot of things going on in their own lives that they don't tell us about, the fact is that our mothers are just as human and vulnerable as we are. They're just a lot better at hiding it. But that shouldn't keep you, as their daughter, from peeking behind the curtain and acknowledging all the work she's done.

I believe it is really important that you let your mother know that you are thankful for them. That you appreciate them. That you want them in your life. Especially once you're old enough to understand that a true, strong relationship requires effort and giving on both sides to succeed.

Going through life and never acknowledging this will almost certainly bring about resentment. No one wants to feel taken advantage of or used and, even if that's not your intention, if you're always the recipient but never the giver, that's what you're doing.

It is easy to take advice from a mother, to take the help when offered, to receive the words of comfort and love. But as daughters, what are we giving back? Do we give back that same measure of love and care? Are we truly there for them, as well, when they need it the most?

Expressing your love, dedication, and gratitude are all very easy things to do. It doesn't require a bouquet of flowers every week. A quick text saying how much you love and appreciate your mother is a great start.

As a daughter, it is also important to let your mother know she did a good job raising you. Do you have to lie and say it was all perfect? Surely not. But a simple, "I loved X, Y, or Z about my childhood and I thank you for that," when all mothers have regrets and things they wish they could change might make all the difference to her.

"A mother is not a person to lean on, but a person to make leaning unnecessary." – Dorothy Canfield Fisher

Sometimes, I will thank my mother for something she did for me, and she'll say, "Oh, you don't have to thank me for that, I'm your mom."

But guess what? Being a mom doesn't mean you *have* to do anything. Sure, we have ideals that many mothers subscribe to, but everything is a choice. And the fact that my mother chooses to treat me with love and kindness, and do special things for me is one I truly appreciate. Not everyone is lucky enough to have that. It's my job to make sure she realizes I'm aware of that fact.

Don't stop with just thanks, though. Take it a step further by returning the favor! If your mother is ever going through a hard time, whether her relationship with her other children is rocky, or maybe her career is becoming overwhelmingly stressful, you can be there for her in ways you've never imagined. You might not be able to wave a magic wand and fix things for her, but just knowing she has you in her corner will help.

Remember, so long as we keep trying, we can never truly fail.

Chapter Objectives...

- ✓ The next time you speak with your mother or daughter, take the time to tell her thank you.

- ✓ Love is a two-way street. A great relationship is give *and* take.

- ✓ You can be there for your mother in ways you've never imagined.

Chapter 13

Be A Mother. Be A Daughter. Be A Friend.

When daughters are young, they need so much help navigating through life that mothers need to embrace the traditional role of motherhood and focus on teaching, guiding, discipline, etc. As daughters mature, though, more and more opportunities will arise for a mother to simply be a friend to her daughter.

This comes from learning when to give advice, but also when to stop and take a step back. It can be hard to know when daughters want to make their own decisions and just need an ear to listen instead of someone who will fix things for them. The balance between can be a fine line to walk. We all know that a mother can't be a friend all the time, but being a parent figure all the time may prevent the daughter from trusting her or confiding in her mother out of fear of punishment or concern that she "just won't understand".

Work to find that balance. Listen and process before responding with a "fix" or, worse, a reprimand. The more a mother is able to do that, especially as their daughter moves toward becoming a woman in her own right, the closer that bond will be.

Being a friend, as well as a family member, can also be applied to daughters. Most of the time, it's easier to be the dutiful daughter, the one that is loving towards her mother, but doesn't really see her as a separate person with feelings and a whole other identity outside of "Mom". That's totally normal during childhood. But as a daughter matures, there will be times when she truly can be her mother's closest friend. She can be the one to give advice, be the problem-solver, or just be willing to listen to her mother vent. It's easy for mothers to get stuck in their role as parent and overall knowledge holder. However, as daughters progress and grow, life will also give them opportunities to educate their mothers, to show them a new aspect of life, or even a window into a new generation.

Be open to teaching *and* learning. Be willing to give advice sometimes and, other times, be a shoulder to lean…or cry on! You'll find your bond will be stronger for the effort.

Life Experience: There For Me, by Dawn

As a mother, I've helped Cher through a lot when she was growing up.

If she had a rough day at school, or some other kid was bullying her, I was there with milk and cookies and a warm hug (while silently plotting revenge on the little bastard who hurt her).

If she didn't win at a dance competition, I was there to

remind her how hard she'd worked and that she'd given it her best.

And when some dumb boy broke her heart, I was there to listen (without even reminding her that I told her so...most of the time).

Honestly, though, Cher has helped me many times, as well. In fact, she helped me through one of the most difficult personal times of my life.

When Cher was growing up, I had a female friend I was very, very close to. We would confide in each other, share everything about our day on hour-long calls, and we would try our best to spend time with each other and have a gabfest when our two crazy schedules would allow it.

One day, in a decision that seemed totally out of the blue to me, this friend decided she didn't want to be friends anymore. I had come to rely on this person, and suddenly, she was gone.

I was totally devastated. I couldn't believe that she had been a part of my daily life for so many years, and now we were just supposed to act like strangers.

Unable to understand or process what happened, I called several times and asked her what happened. I wanted desperately to fix the situation, and told her that, whatever I had done wrong, I was sorry for it. Our kids were close in age, our families had a bond. It seemed like a great, big crack in my life, and I was never given a clear reason why it happened. Not having an answer or a best female friend to talk to about it really sort of broke me.

It was like a poison inside me, and I needed to let it out,

mourn, and weep. It was then that I turned to my *very* best friend, Cher.

She'd known something was wrong for days, and I could tell that it was really bothering her that I was trying to hide it and act like everything was okay. It was then that I realized it wasn't a weakness to share my pain with my daughter. It was a blessing that I was able to.

So I sat her down and explained what had happened and how I was feeling. Cher helped me talk through the whole situation, and really gave me the comfort I needed to move on. She reminded me that I can't change people or require that they treat me a certain way. All I can do is control my own behavior and the way I treat others. If I felt I had been a good friend, and had apologized for any transgressions that I was aware of, the ball wasn't in my court anymore. I had done my part, and if the other woman didn't want to tell me what the issue was, there was no way to mend the relationship. I had to move on and let it go.

And I did.

Even though I'm the mother, sometimes every woman needs another woman to lean on. A best friend who can hold your chin up for you when you don't have the strength. And sometimes, that woman?

Is your beloved daughter.

"The more a daughter knows the details of her mother's life, the stronger the daughter." – Anita Diamant

Life Experience: Shots, by Cher

The time in my life came when I was getting married, and to say I was excited would be a huge understatement.

I was off the rails!

Of course, my mother was so involved with the planning and the process that it all went off without a hitch. She was intent on making sure everything was perfect on the day of the wedding. She truly wanted me to have my dream day. From picking out my dress, to every little detail in the décor. We did the food tasting together and she even came to help pick out the centerpieces. I couldn't honestly imagine creating everything for this wedding without my mother's close attention to detail and, of course, her loving support.

So, when it came to my bachelorette party, I thought it would be so nice if she shared in that experience, too. I knew it was a little unconventional, but I couldn't imagine celebrating without her. She has always been my very best friend and I knew it was going to be a very special experience I was never going to forget, so I wanted her there to experience that with me.

I was a little hesitant to tell all my friends that my mother would be joining us for the party, but my fears were for nothing. It turned out that they were psyched to have her come! They all knew how close we were, but they also thought she was a lot of fun and believed having her there would only add to the experience. When the day finally came, we all met at the airport and boarded a plane to Las Vegas. When we arrived in Nevada and checked in to our hotel, we were given two adjoining rooms. It was me, my mother, and one friend in one room, and the other girls in the other. Before I went up to the rooms, the girls took the time to decorate and it was an amazing surprise that started the weekend off perfectly.

For our first night there, we all got dressed up and went out. I dressed in a white shirt and the girls and my mom dressed in light blue matching bridesmaid tanks. She even showed my friends the right way to wear a push-up bra and I thought it was hilarious that my friends were asking my mom for fashion advice. As we headed down The Strip, my friends started taking photos along the way like they were the paparazzi and I was a famous movie star. It all made me feel like a queen for a day.

We went out for a fabulous dinner and then to a club

afterwards to dance the night away.

Half of me wondered whether my mother was just going to go out to dinner with us and then go back to the hotel to go to bed early, but she delighted everyone when she came out to the club ready to boogie.

At the club, the bass was pumping, everyone was either drinking or dancing, and I knew my friends were concerned my mom would think it was too loud or get irritated by the crowd.

Clearly, they didn't know Dawn Hubsher that well, lol.

Her baby girl was about to get hitched, and she was along for the ride, whatever that entailed. And she was going to enjoy every minute of it with me.

That's the best thing about my mother — she knows when to be a mother and also when to be a true friend. And that night, it was all about our friendship.

Once the bouncer saw that we were having a bachelorette party, we were given a private table with bottle service in the VIP section. Once we were in plain view of everyone at the club, random guys started coming by to chat us up. A couple of my friends were single, so we innocently socialized with the nicer guys and sent the losers packing. But when I turned away for two seconds to take a picture with one of the girls, I turned back around to find some guy hitting on my mom!

I knew she could take care of herself, so I just watched with a bemused smile.

Dawn Hubsher, slaying it in Vegas!

Her admirer was clearly hanging on to her every word as she talked and, after a long while, I couldn't help but move closer to eavesdrop.

"You're not driving home, are you, Nate?" she was saying.

The guy, apparently named Nate, shook his head. "No, I took an Uber here."

"Good. Make sure you drink lots of water and stay hydrated."

Apparently, all the mothering she'd put on hold for this trip had come bubbling out onto poor Nate. I had to cover my mouth with my hand to keep from cracking up.

Still, they talked for the next twenty minutes, thick as thieves, and by the time they were done, he stepped away with a big grin.

"So tell me if I got all this down," he said, ticking off on his fingers, "find a nice girl with good values. Compliment her personality, not just her appearance. Get a look at her mother before you pop the question, because that's your future. Make sure she's not a gold-digger. Oh! And if she's rude to waitresses or doesn't tip, dump her."

"Bingo," my mom said with a proud nod.

He shook his head in awe. "I came by to try to get your number, but you seriously give better advice than my mom."

At that, my mother turned toward the rest of us and shot us

a big wink. "Remember that, girls. I'm like King Solomon. Old and wise."

Her new friend and his boys trailed off, maybe to test out his new knowledge, and a few minutes later, a tray of shots was delivered to our table.

"These are on Nate."

My mother was positively tickled at the gesture, but stood there uncertainly as she looked down. I picked up mine and handed one to my mother, who looked like she wasn't sure whether to drink it or toss it over her shoulder for good luck. I couldn't help but ask her if she'd ever had a shot before, and she admitted she hadn't.

So there we were, mother and daughter, 30 years apart, licking salt off our hands and pounding Mom's first shot together. As I gagged and made my usual sour-puss shot face, I looked over at my mom, who was wearing a big smile -my idol.

I think back on that shot as the moment things really shifted into high gear. Because not a tipsy hour later, we found ourselves walking into a male strip club, Mom in tow.

The second the guys saw me in white next to all my girls, we were tugged up towards the stage and given a front row table, right in the middle of the action.

And, phew, was there action!

Oiled up, muscular guys shimmying what their mama's gave them and grinding on the stage. My mom, despite never having seen a naked guy in person besides my dad, of course, was screaming right along with the rest of us.

I shouldn't have been surprised when a burly "cop" announced into the microphone that one of the women at our table had been naughty and it was his job to make sure she wasn't going to give them any trouble...and then proceeded to jump down and stand right in front of my mom.

"Do you have any concealed weapons?" he asked, cocking his hands on his lean hips.

My mom stared, wide-eyed, at the banana hammock just inches from her face and then shook her head before meeting his gaze.

"No, Officer, but you sure do."

"A Mother is she who can take the place of all others but whose place no one else can take." – Cardinal Mermillod

Getting the chance to have these experiences together as a mother-daughter is so important because I'll be able to look

back in life and not just remember my friends being there with me for the fun times, but more importantly, my mom.

There is a time when you are a mother to your daughter, but another time when you can just be her best friend. During that party, I didn't need her to mother me, or encourage me to go to bed by midnight. I needed a friend who was willing to experience it all with me. And she did that. Right down to the banana hammock.

"No matter how old she may be, sometimes a girl just needs her mom." – Cardinal Mermillod

Chapter Objectives...

- ✓ There will be times when a mother will need to be the mother, but there are also opportunities for a mother to simply be a friend to her daughter.

- ✓ There are plenty of opportunities that arise that allow a daughter to be the one to help her mother through a tough time.

- ✓ Strive to go through each new experience together.

Chapter 14

Tending To The Bond,
Even When It Seems Broken

❦

A Mother-Daughter Relationship Isn't Always Great

No relationship is sunshine and rainbows all the time, no matter what people might try to portray on social media. There will be times when the bond you have with your daughter is going to be strained. Something is going to happen where the two of you just don't agree. It might feel like you just keep hitting the same wall over and over again. But the breaking point comes the moment you focus more on being right in a given situation than you do on the dedication you have to the relationship with your mother or daughter.

Mothers, you're going to have to let your daughters learn life lessons the hard way sometimes, even though you're trying your best to prevent them from making a big mistake. They need to be able to learn and grow, and sometimes the only way to do it is to carve their own path. Cheer their successes, regardless, and be there to help them up if they fall and need help finding their way again.

Most of all? Try to avoid the "I told you so" if you can help it!

And daughters, if you're going to go against your mother's wishes, be willing to accept both the triumphs and the failures. Be humble when you're proven right, and admit it when your mother was right all along.

"Words are not enough to express the unconditional love that exists between a mother and a daughter."
– Caitlin Houston

Life Experience: When The Bond Is Strained, by Cher

In high school, I started dating a guy named Mike. I felt a connection that I hadn't felt with any other guy that I had dated previously. He went to a different high school than me and was a year older, too. Even though he was still in high school, he had his own apartment and had a job on top of going to school. Now that I look back, he was actually pretty mature for his age, in that sense. We started dating pretty soon after my MTV *My Super Sweet 16* episode released. The show had been a big hit and, at the time, everyone in my area was talking about 'the girl on the show'.

Mike and I ended up dating for about a year, on and off. But, if I'm being honest, the reason we were "off" sometimes was largely due to my mom.

She hated him.

Like, you know how people who hate olives make a big deal about how gross they are?

To my mother, Mike was olives.

She couldn't stand the sight of him. Whenever I mentioned his name, she'd give a disappointed sniff and turn away. And she barely managed to be polite the handful of times I brought him around.

She never could give me a reason why she disliked him so much. Her only reasoning was that she felt he was dating me for "my money". I got where she was coming from, with the success of the show and all, but it also didn't ring true. After all, he was the one with a job and to be honest, he paid for all of our dates. But no matter how I tried to reason with her, she still insisted that he wasn't the type of guy I should end up with, and she was sure he liked me for the wrong reasons.

This, of course, made me extremely upset because they barely knew each other and the times he did meet her, Mike was always very nice to her. It was infuriating. I was only in high school, I wasn't looking to get married, I was 16 going on 17. Despite my protests, though, she kept reminding me that "you never know who you fall in love with or when it might happen" and she didn't want me to fall in love so young and end up marrying someone who wasn't right for me long-term.

Because she didn't like him for me, it put a lot of stress on my relationship with her. Despite our long-time policy of honesty and openness, during that time period, I felt backed into a corner. If I wanted to spend time with this guy (who'd done nothing wrong to deserve her disdain), I had no choice but to lie. It was that, or break up with him for no real reason, when I still cared about him and wanted to be with him.

It was a miserable position to be put in and I resented my mom for putting me there.

I remember wanting to meet up with Mike on a school night and telling my mother I was going to my friend's house to study. We weren't even doing anything scandalous, just enjoying each other's company. On those nights we'd go sit at the beach to watch the sunset and simply talk.

The few times my mom found out what I'd been really doing, she would be furious and yell at me for lying and sneaking around. At the time, though, I really didn't feel I had a choice.

It was a difficult time for my mother and I, and I could definitely feel the bond beginning to fray.

Later that year, I went away to a summer program at a distant college. While I was away, I realized for myself that, going forward, I wanted a partner who was more ambitious and had other qualities that were important to me that Mike didn't have. Being away from home for six weeks also made me realize that I wanted to be with someone who could be close with my family, as well.

On top of that, when I returned home, I found out that Mike hadn't been faithful and we ended up splitting. It was a very hard, back and forth type of break up that seemed to drag on and on. When I moved to college, he even ended up moving there, too and tried to rekindle our flame. But, by then, I'd realized my mom was right all along.

He just wasn't right for me.

But does that mean I was wrong for digging in my heels? I don't think so. I needed to have that relationship with Mike because it taught me about love. It let me see what was important in a relationship for me. And if I learned something…a valuable lesson (and one that eventually led to me knowing it was *right* when I found my soul mate and husband) then was it really a mistake at all?

I don't think so.

Despite eventually coming to the same conclusion as my mother, it had to be on my terms and not hers. If not, I would've resented her and I might never have learned about the type of man I *did* want in my life.

This was a really tough time between me and my mom, and it really didn't have to be that way. I was sneaking around, lying, and doing something she didn't approve of. I know she just wanted what was best, but I believe what was best would have been to just let me be a kid without focusing on my future for once.

Not that she should've fawned all over him and said he was great if that wasn't how she actually felt. But I wished she would've stepped back and not put so much pressure on me to do what she wanted me to do and respected my choice.

Don't push your will onto your daughter to the point that

she ends up lying to you or sneaking around, unless her behavior is truly unsafe or destructive. Be there for your daughter even if you don't like the person she's with. That's the way to maintain a strong bond, through it all.

And if the crap hits the fan and he proves to be every bit as bad as you knew he was?

She'll know you're in her corner to help pick up the pieces.

"A mother's love for her child is like nothing else in the world. It knows no laws, no pity. It dares all things and crushes down remorselessly all that stands in its path."
– Agatha Christie

Life Experience: Never Wonder 'What If?', by Cher

Growing up, I always wanted to be an actress. It was my childhood dream. I remember watching shows on Disney or Nickelodeon and being so upset that I never had the opportunity to audition.

In elementary school, I was the lead in all my school plays and my acting teacher always told my mom and me, "Get her headshots, she needs to act!" Unfortunately, though, I grew up in an area where acting really wasn't big and there were hardly any auditions. I remember going to sleep crying because I couldn't figure out how to make my dreams come true. I knew that I needed to start acting at a young age and that it would be exponentially harder to break into the industry the older I got.

But, one day, a very big agent was in town from Los Angeles looking for new clients. My mom took me to meet him and I performed a monologue for him, which he provided. After I was done, his mouth dropped open.

And, I remember this part like it was yesterday...

He wrote two letters on a piece of paper and circled them:

L.

A.

He proceeded to tell my mom that I had such a gift and really needed to be in Los Angeles.

"Cher will make it in this industry," he had said.

This was it. I had finally proven to my mom that I was meant to do this!

But even as I was mentally packing my bags, my mom was already shaking her head.

"Honey, I can't just leave your dad and brothers to move to L.A. with you. That's not reasonable."

"Can we at least go for a summer and see what happens?" I begged.

My mom, again, explained she couldn't just pick up and move away with me and leave her other kids behind. That wouldn't be right. I wasn't deterred, though. I asked to go live at an acting school in L.A., but my mom, being the protective mother she is, would never allow such a thing.

For years after, I tried everything I could to change her mind, and even turned to my dad for his help. But they stood firm. I was to finish school, go to college, and after that I could do whatever I wanted. I was stuck. As I got older, I tried begging for a gap year between high school and college to give acting a shot, but I didn't have any money and had already been accepted into a great college. In the end, I was forced to follow their plans for me or face a lot of struggles and obstacles I wasn't ready to face.

To this day, I always wished I had the opportunity to go as a kid. I know child acting isn't always the best lifestyle, but it really was my passion, and it felt like an ache that never really went away.

I made it through college, with the goal of going out to L.A. the second I graduated. What I didn't realize is that I'd meet the love of my life there, and my goals would change. I met my now husband and fell head over heels for him.

After college, we got engaged and moved to Tampa, Florida together where he pursued his medical degree. I found myself working as a nurse and as a professional cheerleader on the side. Life was really good. I married my best friend and had two jobs I loved.

But a piece of me was still missing.

I had followed my husband to pursue his dreams, but I still never felt like I had the opportunity to pursue mine the way I always wanted. So, while in Tampa, I enrolled myself in acting classes and started studying. By doing so, the urge to go to L.A. came back. I knew in my heart I needed to go or I would always regret not following my dream.

I discussed all of this with my husband, and being my rock, soul mate, and support system, he told me to go for it. He said we would see each other when we could and we would talk every day on the phone. He told me to go until I felt like I'd done what I needed to do and was ready to come home. I felt so blessed to have someone who understood me and really wanted to support me so I didn't have regrets.

Next, I had to tell my parents. Needless to say, they were stunned. They said I was going to ruin my relationship with my husband. Since we were newly married, they were very concerned that me moving away for a bit of time would cause us to grow apart. They loved my husband like a son and were so scared that my decision would jeopardize our relationship.

They were extremely upset, even after I explained to them that this was something we'd discussed at length and had agreed on. Just like before, they told me not to go. But this time, I was grown. And, even though they tried everything they could think of to stop me, I listened to my gut and moved to L.A. with the idea that I would stay at least five months to give it a real shot.

I was going to see this through. No regrets.

I'm happy to report that, once she knew my decision had been made and I left, my mother did support me while I was out in L.A. She would always help me figure out what to wear for each audition and would even help me practice my lines. Knowing she didn't really love me being there, I appreciated that she at least made the effort. Our bond stayed strong because, despite her fighting me on it, she didn't abandon me when I didn't follow her advice.

It wasn't easy being away from my husband, though. And it

wasn't easy breaking into the industry since I didn't have any real past acting experience. I did my very best, and, in that short amount of time, I accomplished a lot!

I was in an 8-week long theatrical play, a short film, and landed supporting roles in two feature films. I also booked a theatrical and commercial agent while I was there. I was meeting many directors, producers, and other actors, and really started to make a name for myself while I was there.

One of the feature films that I was cast in while I was in L.A. was actually filming in my hometown of Tampa. I couldn't believe that I got cast in L.A. all to just go back to Florida! It was like the world was trying to tell me something. Because, after this whole experience, I realized I loved acting...but I loved my life with my husband more.

I was so proud of everything I accomplished in such a short amount of time, but boy, the hustle was real! Acting took everything out of me. Every night I was going out late and networking so I could meet the next person who could help my career. It just wasn't a lifestyle that I felt would be healthy long-term for my relationship. My husband was so supportive, but I felt I was basically living two lives, and it just wasn't fair. I made my commitment to my husband the day I said, "I do" and I was going to stand by that commitment. Only now, I could do it with a whole heart and the knowledge that I'd tried.

I'd followed my dreams and found that my dreams had changed somewhere along the way.

Although I was also happy in L.A., what I was most happy about was having that opportunity to try. I stopped having

regrets, and I felt like I finally succeeded. I was so thankful that my husband supported me and I feel like we have a much better relationship now because of it.

You can't go through life always wishing and dreaming. We are the creators of our own destiny and we are the only ones that should be holding ourselves back. Moving to L.A. when I did was the best decision I made for my relationship because it allowed me to try, to move on, and stop always wondering, "What if?"

"The purpose of life is to live it, to taste experience to the utmost, to reach out eagerly and without fear for newer and richer experience." – Eleanor Roosevelt

Chapter Objectives...

✓ No matter the state in which a mother-daughter relationship is in, it can always be tended to.

✓ The breaking point comes when you focus more on being right than on your relationship with your mother or daughter.

✓ Don't let anyone stop you from trying to attain your goals. If they truly love you, your relationship will survive it.

Chapter 15

Remember: There Is No Perfect Blueprint For Being A Mom

Regardless of the parenting classes mothers take, the books they read, or the advice they exchange with other women, there is still no one, surefire path to being a good mom.

Some mothers worry about being the perfect role models for their daughters. But you know how you truly demonstrate to your daughter how to be 'perfect'? By showing others the same dedication and kindness you give your daughter. If you want your daughter to be compassionate and an includer, then be one yourself!

Being a role model doesn't mean being 'perfect'. Reveal your own mistakes and flaws. By doing so, you show your daughter that you're human, too. We all know that sometimes life doesn't go as planned. There are days that you will manage to get perfectly cut PB&Js into that lunchbox with a side of neatly cut carrot sticks and milk money to go with it. And then there are days when you forget to even stick two bucks in her pocket for pizza day. Let her see you roll with the punches, and still come out standing. Let her see that sometimes you are hurt or sad or angry, but that you still press on and prevail, no matter how tough things get.

And most of all, remind her that she, too, can be a super woman without having to be Super Woman.

"Even on the days you feel like you are failing, look around, I promise your kids still think you are the best mom in the universe." – Julie Clark

Life Experience: There Is No Textbook, by Dawn

I never babysat when I was young, so I really didn't know anything about babies when I became a mother. In fact, I didn't even know how to diaper my children when my first son was born (and I'm so glad there were no iPhones back then to record my efforts, because I was terrible at it!)

But the one thing becoming a mother forces you to do is to learn. You experience things you never thought possible in your life. You discover your inner strengths, and even your deeper weaknesses. It's lifechanging, terrifying, and amazing, all at the same time. Nothing can prepare you for that, no matter how much you read or talk to other people. All you can do is grab the reins, hold on tight for the ride, and try your best.

There were so many times while I was raising Cher that life just wasn't easy, no matter how blessed I felt at having a daughter. At each stage of her life (and in our relationship), it took some adjusting on both of our ends.

When she was an infant, she had to adjust to the fact that she wasn't in the womb anymore and I had to adjust to the fact that I would never get a full night's sleep again.

When she was a toddler, I had to adjust to the fact that she was a nudist in the making, and she had to adjust to the fact that there were times and places where she had to wear clothes…until she ripped them off, at least.

When she was in Kindergarten, I had to adjust to the fact that she thought the world was her canvas and she had to adjust to the fact that, while I wanted to encourage her creativity, my living room walls were off limits.

And as she grew older and found her independence, the types of struggles changed but it didn't get a whole lot easier. I still felt like I was flying without a net. I would worry about her choices, who she was with, or what she was doing. She would steal my clothes and either never put them back in my closet or wear something, stain it, and pretend she never wore it. There was also a period where she got super sassy and used to talk back to me. On one hand, it drove me nuts. On the other, it made me proud that she was so strongminded. I wanted to raise a leader. Someone who isn't afraid to stand up for herself and tell it like it is. I'm so glad she turned out to be all that and more. *But,* those same traits made her hard to communicate with at points.

Because I'd taught her to be tough, when she wanted to do something, she would be stubborn and dig her heels in (even with me. Not what I was going for!)

Because I'd taught her to be honest, she could err on the side of being a bit *too* blunt (even with me! Again, not my intention, because who wants to hear that their new dress makes them look stumpy or that the pasta salad they'd made for their Fourth of July party tastes like dirty socks?)

Hey, maybe I didn't do it all perfectly, but I did it the best way I knew how. Like Old Blue Eyes used to say, I did it *my way*. And you know what? I'm proud to have raised a strong, independent woman rather than one who is going to bend to the will of others and b.s. her way through life by yessing other people to death.

If Cher wants something, she's going to go after it, whether I agree or not. If I ask Cher a question, I might not like her answer, but I'll know it's her honest opinion. Those are valuable assets in both a daughter AND a friend, and I wouldn't change her for the world.

Life Experience: Strength of Character, by Cher

After having two sons, my mom was so happy to finally have a girl that she immediately started dressing me up and would find us matching outfits. She loved when we dressed alike and, from a young age, I started to love it, too.

As I got older, though, I realized that my friends' moms didn't look like mine. They dressed like typical moms. Lots of Anne Taylor clothes for the working mothers, and high-waisted jeans paired with denim shirts bedazzled with roosters or flowers on them for the stay at home crew.

That was…not my mom in the 90's.

To give you a mental picture, we're talking somewhere between Peg Bundy from Married With Children and Fran Drescher in the Nanny, only a little classier. Dawn Hubsher didn't own a pair of flats, and that included her bedroom slippers. Her favorite color?

BLACK.

She moved with the times, and when I got to be a teenager, she was the height of fashion…for a teenager.

More than once, people would ask us if we were sisters, and I'm not going to lie: back in the day that was something that really started to bother me. It felt awkward to explain to complete strangers or people I was introducing my mother to that she was my mother and not my sister. I remember one time, she was dropping me off at a party, and everyone made such a big deal about how cool she looked. I got all in my hormonal teenage feelings about it and wound up near tears.

When I got home, I flat out asked her why she couldn't dress like a normal mom instead of someone so young. Her honest, heartfelt response sort of rocked me back on my heels.

She said, "I dress the way that makes me feel the most comfortable and beautiful, Cher. And I hope one day when you're my age you have the confidence to do the same."

Well played, Mom. Well played.

I'm not going to say I always loved it, but I damn sure respected it and I never asked her about it again. And, once I understood her viewpoint, I even started to embrace us dressing alike again.

She would buy the cutest outfits and I would raid her closest prior to going out at night or to friends' houses. After her constantly finding my clothes in her closest or hers in mine, she started just buying two of everything. I loved that because, when I got older and would come home to visit, I'd have adorable outfits waiting for me that I never would have found on my own.

Despite our similar tastes and love of dressing alike, there were some occasions where we definitely didn't want that to happen...

This one time, I showed up to a friend's wedding in this adorable, yellow cocktail dress that my mom had gotten for me a few months prior. As I was walking in, a friend stopped me and said, "Did you just get here? I could have sworn I saw you at the cocktail table earlier!"

Confused, I just said that yes, I'd just arrived, and went along my merry way.

All of a sudden, I see a girl in a yellow cocktail dress that looked just like me from afar. Long dark hair with ironed waves, same build and everything. For a second, I thought it was a mirror, but as I moved closer, I realized it definitely wasn't.

A few seconds later, I am standing face to face with my mom, both of us red-faced and horrified.

The first time we don't discuss what we were going to wear to a big event, and we show up looking like twins.

I wanted to run home and change but the doors were closing and the wedding bells were beginning to ring. It was too late. Rather than let it ruin our night, we decided to rock the twin thing and, to our surprise, we both wound up having a lot of fun with it.

There was another time that things got weird, though. A couple years back, my parents, me and my husband were all invited to the same cookout. Jared had to work for part of the day, so he planned to meet us there. My mother had taken a liking to a sundress that she'd seen in my closet and asked if she could wear it that day, and of course, I said yes. She changed clothes and we headed to the party, ready to have a nice day in the sunshine.

Imagine her surprise when she snuck off to a quiet corner to make a quick phone call only to feel a smack on the butt that had her turning around ready to slap somebody. There stood my poor husband, realizing a few seconds too late that he'd been deceived by the dress and he'd smacked the wrong cheeks!

Of course, they wound up laughing about it, and my dad teases him to this day, but I'm not sure poor Jared will ever fully recover from the trauma of slapping his mother-in-law's butt.

As for me and my mom, we don't twin all the time nowadays, but we still do love to match when we go out. And even when we're not twinning, we're still both partial to the same styles, colors, and patterns. At least we never have to worry about showing up and feeling out of place because there will always be someone else there (maybe even your twin) to make us seem totally in style!

Every mother and daughter has a thing, and dressing alike is ours.

Now that I'm an adult, it's also a point of pride for me that she looks so great and likes to dress in a youthful way. Plus, bonus: I get to raid her closet. When I go home to visit Florida, I can literally go with just my toothbrush if need be, because I have access to a full array of trendy, stylish clothes in my size at my disposal! Not only that, but clothing has also come to be another great way for us to bond. My mother enjoys shopping for me, and since we both enjoy the same style of clothes, I can send my mother outfits in return. We could spend hours shopping together. I'm glad my mother didn't take offense to my comment about her choice of styles when I was younger because I see how much joy she has from wearing the clothes she feels good in. More importantly, though, she taught me by example not to let anyone (not even your beloved, well-meaning daughter!) tell you how to dress or who to be.

Dawn Hubsher may not have had a How To book or a blueprint to follow. In fact, she may have winged it for the most part, but there's no denying it; She's been a great role model for me and has taught me to be strong and have confidence in all that I do.

Which is good, as confidence and strength are things I'm definitely going to need in the next few months, because I have some BIG NEWS!!!

Surprise, Surprise!

On October 23rd, I found out that I, Cher Hubsher, was pregnant.

I couldn't believe it!

I had seen a psychic about a year ago who told me that if I wasn't careful, I would get pregnant towards the end of 2018. Well, sure enough, it happened! It was the first time my husband and I ever didn't use protection. We were planning to start trying in November, but things got a bit carried away. My mom always told me she felt me as soon as she conceived, and I honestly felt the same way with this baby. I knew I was pregnant the night it happened.

I felt my body shift and change and, very quickly, started

having vivid dreams that were totally atypical of my usual dreams. I decided to take a home test to see if I was pregnant. It was 5 days early, which I knew may not even show yet, but I was sure and wanted that confirmation.

Sure enough, for the first time ever, a big plus sign came into view. I was *so* excited, I wanted to call my husband and mom right away, but I also wanted that moment when I told them to be very special.

For my husband, I planned a whole day on the beach where he thought he was helping me take photos for my NYC Wingwoman website. Earlier that morning, I told the photographer what was really going on and to play along.

Halfway through the photo shoot, the photographer gave us both small chalk boards and had us stand back to back so that we couldn't see what the other would write. The first thing he did was tell us to write down what superhero the other person was. We each wrote something down and, at his direction, took three steps apart and turned around at the same time to show each other. My husband said I was Wonder Woman and I wrote down that he was my Superman. We then went back to back again and this time (as previously planned) the photographer told us to write down what we want in our future together. We then wrote it down and took three steps apart and at the same time showed each other our chalk board. His said, "A family".

And mine?

Said, "You're going to be a daddy!"

He was so shocked and excited. That moment is one of my best all-time memories and one I can't wait to share with our baby.

I wanted to tell my mom in a very special way, too. We happened to be filming a reality TV show at the time for TLC, and my husband and I planned to tell our whole family when we were all together at Thanksgiving. I knew I couldn't tell my mom over the phone as it just wouldn't be as special as getting to tell her in person. I also knew I had to get her alone and tell her before everyone else because it wouldn't be as special for her. I mean, she was finally going to be a grandma, or 'Mimi' — something she always wanted to be called. So, even though keeping this secret was difficult, I knew it would be worth it in the end.

On Thanksgiving Day, while all the boys were outside playing and my mom and I were preparing the Thanksgiving meal, I just couldn't hold it in anymore. I had her sit down and I gave her a very special mug that I had ordered for her. It said, "Only the best moms get promoted to Mimi" and inside the mug she found my pregnancy test along with my first ultrasound.

She immediately burst into tears, and I quickly followed suit. To say she was excited would be an understatement! She kissed my pee stick! And she still has that pee-stick in a box in her dresser drawer and I'm pretty sure she would've actually had it bronzed if she could've!

It was one of the happiest days of both of our lives, and it felt like we'd come full circle.

As we get to the end of the journey that has been the writing of this book, I can't wait to start the next one as a mother myself. I can only hope to be just as good of a mom to my child as my mother has always been to me!

"A baby is something you carry inside you for nine months, in your arms for three years, and in your heart until the day you die." – Mary Mason

Chapter Objectives...

- ✓ Being a good mother means being a good role model. Try your best and remember, nobody is perfect!

- ✓ There is plenty for mothers to learn when they first become mothers, but there is always something new to learn when it comes to continually being a successful mother.

- ✓ You don't need to be like every other mom to be a great mom.

Bonus Chapter

Read on for bonus material where we discuss moms of multiples, single moms, mother/daughter-in-law relationships, and give a recap of the lessons we've learned!

Welcome to the bonus chapter! We are truly excited for you to have read this far into the book. We hope you learned something along the way and enjoyed the little insights into our lives throughout the years.

That said, we understand that every mother-daughter bond is different. In an effort to include all types of relationships, we interviewed an array of mothers and daughters with circumstances that were different than our own. Some were mothers with multiple daughters, others were single mothers or mothers of adopted daughters. We took the best bits of wisdom from those conversations and compiled them for this bonus section. But the starting place for all of us is the same, no matter the condition or circumstance of your relationship. If you want to strengthen that bond, the time to start is *today*!

Before diving into the different family dynamics that may

affect just how you, in particular, strengthen the mother-daughter relationship you currently have, let's first recap some of what we read and give you a simple, 8-step process for strengthening a mother-daughter relationship that applies to the universal love that mothers have for their daughters, and the love daughters will always have for their mothers.

Strengthening And Mending A Mother-Daughter Relationship

1) Improve Communication

The surest way to improve any relationship is to keep lines of communication open. This can start with just a few text messages here and there to remind your mother or daughter that you love and care about them. If texting isn't your thing, then a letter works, too! The fact that you took the time to find a stamp and mail it is both touching and thoughtful.

After you feel comfortable with texting or sending letters, start calling your mother or daughter more frequently. Instead of just once a month, start making a routine out of calling every Sunday evening to chat. Talk about your week, and then ask questions to get some insight into what's going on in their life, as well.

No matter what method you use to increase the amount of communication between yourself and your mother or daughter, make sure that you're both talking *and* listening. Modern technology might make it very easy to stay in touch with our loved ones, but it's up to us to determine the quality of each conversation. Are your words positive, or are you complaining about one thing or another? Try to also keep the conversations positive, and only bring in the negative if you're willing to receive advice and help in return.

2) Spend Quality Time

Having good communication practices is key to a strong mother-daughter relationship, but you also have to take the time to spend quality time together. It can sometimes be hard when the mother and daughter don't live close to one another, but that makes it all the more special when you set time aside to travel to see each other and spend time with each other.

When you do get together with your mother or daughter, make sure you plan special activities together, whether that is going out shopping or staying in and baking all day. Whatever you choose to do while visiting, make sure you choose to do it together. Watching TV or going to see a movie may not be the best activities because you're not really doing anything memorable and you don't get the opportunity to talk while you're doing it. Instead, plan activities that include action, dialogue, and, of course, teamwork. There is nothing more strengthening to a mother-daughter relationship than when you work together to accomplish something magical. This leads to long lasting memories you'll have fun reminiscing about for years to come.

3) Include Often

No matter what your day looks like, you can find one way or another to include your mother or daughter in on the experience. This can be inviting them over to spend time with you or your family, or just simply taking a quick selfie of you in your new outfit, or at the gym and sending it to your mother or daughter to show them what you're up to.

This is especially important during a life change or milestone. Make sure to find a way to include your mother or daughter in on that adventure! First day at college? Sunrise on day one of your first trip overseas? Or how about grandbaby's first steps? Take two seconds and snap a pic. Your mom or daughter will thank you for it.

Including your mother or daughter into the big and small aspects of your life demonstrates to them how much you are truly dedicated to them and truly want them in your life.

With apps like FaceTime, Snapchat, Instagram and Facebook Live, it's easier than ever to share the most exciting events with those you love when distance is an issue.

Daughters, if Mom doesn't know how to use these apps, teach her! It can be another special thing only the two of you share.

4) Express Your Love Uniquely

Calls, texts and visits are great, and are the backbone of any relationship, but it's also fun being creative. You don't have to do something lavish or expensive, but going out of your way to hand-make a gift for your mom for Mother's Day shows just how much she means to you. Maybe you can get her one of those digital picture frames that scrolls through different pictures that you hand-picked of the two of you. Or maybe you could send her a playlist of the showtunes you guys used to sing in the car together when you were growing up. Anything that shows you're thinking of them, from showing up to their house with dinner already made and ready to eat or sending a care package when they are sick and overnighting it to them.

There are so many different ways to express to your mother or daughter that you are dedicated to them, care about them, and want them in your life. The goal is to express these feelings in a unique way that truly will strengthen the bond you have with your mother or daughter.

5) Don't Give Up

It's tough growing and maintaining any relationship. It can be even more difficult when the person you are trying to love is hesitant or non-responsive. No matter the condition of your mother-daughter relationship, the most important thing to remember is not to give up. There will be times when you argue with your mother or daughter, but that doesn't mean you throw in the towel. Remember all the good times together and the moments where genuine love was expressed and felt. Rough patches in the relationship will happen, and it's in those moments that having great memories will sustain you.

When you feel like giving up after trying for so long to mend a mother-daughter relationship, remember what you're fighting for. Remember that you love them and deep down inside that they still love you, too. You never know when a certain text, phone call, or email is going to be the one thing that finally helps them move forward as well in the relationship. The important thing is not to hold a grudge or let negative feelings hold you back from experiencing one of the greatest joys in life.

6) Open Up And Be Honest

Now that you've increased the quality of communication with your mother or daughter and have made a point to include them in your life and do special things together, it's time to go a step further. You do that by opening up to them and being completely honest. That will allow you to work through any past hurts and avoid future ones. And, remember; You can say what you mean without being mean!

When you share your experiences honestly, you also allow the ones you love to help when you need it, and are then able to help them, as well. You can always be there for your mother or daughter as she faces life's biggest trials, and the best way to do so is to be honest with her and be open about your own life experiences.

7) Cherish Every Moment

Life is short. Tomorrow isn't promised, and yesterday is already in the past. All we are truly guaranteed is right now. So, right now, remember to cherish every moment you get to spend with your mother or daughter. Whether that's through a phone call or getting to spend actual face-to-face time with them, it's important to express the love we have for our mother or daughter whenever we can.

Don't procrastinate. If you feel like your mother-daughter relationship isn't as strong as it should be, then take the time to fix that. There is nothing more heartbreaking than regret.

8) Rain Will Come So Have An Umbrella Ready!

Though we'd like to think that nothing will ever happen to the ones we love, sometimes, things happen. The last thing we want when an emergency arises and we need to fly halfway across the country to be with our mother or daughter is to have a financial obstacle in our way.

If you were lucky enough to have the financial security to save for your daughter's college tuition and now she's at school, keep saving if you can! Put money aside for when the unexpected does happen. Maybe your daughter will wind up getting married at a younger age than you imagined, and will need a little extra help as her family gets started. Or maybe you'll have a little nest egg for her if she winds up expecting a bundle of joy herself.

On the flip side, daughters, start building that nest egg on your end, too! Maybe your mother will fall ill and be unable to afford to pay her mortgage, or lose everything in a house fire or flood. Having that little nest egg of resources can be a life saver for those you love in their time of need. And if not? Then you have a nice little chunk of money put away for the future. Whatever your current financial situation is now, put forth the effort to save even the smallest amounts for when life does happen and teach your daughter to do the same. You don't want to be stuck at home when you'd rather be on the road or on a plane to be closer to your mother or daughter at the last second.

"The love between a mother and daughter is for life."
– Cher Hubsher

Every Mother-Daughter Relationship Is Different

We wish we could provide some formula or equation that would help every mother and daughter. Unfortunately, there isn't a 'one size fits all' method to strengthening and maintaining the bond between a mother and her daughter. Instead, we've tried our best to provide the basics to mending a mother-daughter relationship, or just finding ways to strengthen one over time. Thoughtful and measurable action is the key to a long-lasting relationship with your mother or daughter.

But what if you have two? Or three??

Mothers of Multiples

Making time for your daughter and putting that bond first isn't always easy. Doing it when you have more than one daughter makes it even harder!

Not only is that mother striving to stay up to date with everything going on in every daughter's life, but she's trying to show dedication and compassion to each of them. It's a juggling act, for sure.

We recommend not only scheduling girls' days (if possible, depending on locations) involving all of you, but also making sure each child has their own "thing" that just she and mom do together. For one daughter, it might be shopping together and dressing alike. For another, it might be sushi and sake night, and for another still, it might be a hike in the woods, or a trip to the beach.

The goal is to make each feel special, while still also tending to the overall family bond and spending time all together.

If you're a daughter with several sisters, we suggest the same. Mom's birthday is coming up? Get everyone together and plan a surprise party. She'll be so excited you went to the effort (and shocked that you managed to pull one over on her, to boot!) But also remember to check in on your own, just to see how she's doing and have some one on one interaction.

As a daughter with sisters, it can also be really great because you can help each other work through tough times with your mother, and also help your mother if she's struggling with one of her daughters.

Sometimes a situation just needs a different perspective or a mediator to help solve the problem.

A quick word about treating each child equally...

One of the hardest parts about raising multiple kids is finding a balance within the family environment where a mother, or even both parents, treats each child equally. Though the bond between a mother and her daughter is like none other, she can have as strong of a bond with her sons and husband. It is simply a different dynamic.

It's very important to make sure to treat all your children fairly. This helps balance the family environment and keeps resentments and insecurities at bay.

That said, every child is different, so our approach is based on being fair. But being fair doesn't mean treating them all the same.

Some kids don't need to be forced to do their homework. They come home, sit down with a snack and get to work because they're hardwired that way. Whereas, others need to be cuffed to the kitchen table and threatened with bodily harm before they'll even pick up a pencil. Should the rules be the same for both or might one require a stronger incentive?

Some kids might be allowed to walk to the bus stop at a young age on their own because they're responsible and you trust that they will do as they're told, not talk to strangers, and get to school in one piece. Others are maybe not mature enough, even at that same age, and would climb into the back of a white van for the promise of a lollipop without even thinking twice!

Now, is it the same or equal that you would let child A walk alone but not child B?

No.

But is it fair?

Based on their personalities and their abilities, we would say it is.

You might have one toddler that eats crayons and another who strips off their diaper and uses the contents to create a monochromatic Jackson Pollack on your wall. Give the Pollack painter the crayons and some paper, and give the other some cut up grapes and read them a story!

As a mom, you've got to think on the fly and more importantly, you have to adapt to each child's needs, personality, and individuality.

Point is, the behavior or needs of one child might demand more attention or alternate actions, and that's okay! There are still plenty of opportunities for mothers to spend quality time with each of her children and instill in them her dedication to them despite their differences.

At the end of the day, all we can do is ensure we're doing our best and being *fair*. When there isn't fairness at home, it will cause animosity and sibling rivalry. Not only will the children start fighting against each other, but they will all fight each other for their parents' attention and love.

A good way to assess this is ask yourself the tough questions:

Are you treating each child fairly?

Do you perhaps subconsciously have a closer relationship with one child compared to the others?

If the answers lead you to the unpleasant realization that you are giving one child preferential treatment, it's time to nip that in the bud, ASAP. Make a conscious effort to change it.

Treating everyone fairly is an important dynamic of the family lifestyle because it allows children to grow up in a stable environment. Siblings are then more likely to get along and have a closer relationship not only with their parents, but with each other, as well.

Adopted Mother and Daughter

No matter if a daughter is born to a mother or adopted into her life one way or another, the mother-daughter bond can still be created and nurtured the same way. That said, sometimes, when an older girl is adopted into the family, it may take some time to create a bond with her. The mother is then given the task to make sure her new daughter feels included; that she feels not only loved, but also safe and respected.

Mothers of adopted daughters, don't ever give up. There is nothing more triumphant than hearing your adopted daughter call you her mother and really feel that connection. Your adopted daughter might act out at first, and it might take time for her to not only see your love for her, but trust it and believe in it fully.

Be patient. Be loving. Be kind.

To daughters that have been adopted, we understand there might be a deep hurt from the idea of not being with or wanted by your birth mother. But remember, it's very likely that your birth mother loved you and could not provide the life you deserved at that time. And please remember that your adopted mother chose you to be her daughter, and that she longed for the day when she could have a daughter just like you.

If both of you are willing to put in the work and effort, you can reap the same benefits as mothers and daughters who have had a lifetime together. We've seen it with friends of ours, and it's beautiful!

Life Experience: Mother-In-Law, by Cher

I was so lucky to have the best mother-in-law that a girl could ever ask for. She was the kindest, strongest, and most fearless woman that I have ever met.

When a girl falls in love with a boy, she has no control over what his family is going to be like. When she marries him, she hopes that they will be loving and welcoming. However, she enters that family for the boy she fell head-over-heels for. As a mom, you have the ability to keep your family close by welcoming that daughter-in-law with open arms. I can tell you from experience, that warm-welcoming feeling is the best feeling in the world, knowing that you can always be yourself with his family and not feel like you have to put on a show for them. That same feeling is what will allow your son to always stay close with his family, never resent them, or have built up anger or be fed angry words by his wife. Remember the saying, "A son is a son until he finds a wife, but a daughter is yours for the rest of your life?" I promise you that it does not have to be that way. In fact, since Jared and I have been married, I encouraged him to be even closer with his mom because I saw how wonderful she is and I loved having her as a big part of our life.

Amy, my mother-in-law, was diagnosed with triple-negative breast cancer a year before our wedding, a terrible cancer that she had fought for six years. She was my role model and biggest inspiration as she continuously fought hard to survive more than any person that I have ever met. Anytime she was told she needed a new surgery or new treatment plan, she was ready to try her best and live as long as possible so that she could be there for her loved ones. After her double mastectomy, I flew to Florida and took care of her. Everything from changing her drains, showering her, changing her gauze and cleaning her wounds, I was more than happy to be there because I loved her as a mom and wanted her to be strong again.

When I began writing this section of the book, I was sitting in hospice next to my mother-in-law as she took her last few breaths. It was a truly devastating time, but even my pain could not detract from how blessed I felt to have her in my life. The only memories I have with her over the past ten years are ones that warm my heart. From the moment Jared introduced me to his mom, we had this marvelous connection. She was a dentist and owned her own practice. She had me come in for cleanings and re-worked my smile into pearly whites. She would take me out to lunches, shopping days (she loved to shop), and we would talk on the phone for hours. She always wanted to be a part of my life and she showed that with her open communication and non-judgmental attitude.

When I first started visiting my mother-in-law, I would always dress up. I felt I didn't want her to see all the blemishes I had or imperfections, but she would always tell me, "You don't need to wear makeup or straighten your hair." I then started really being myself around her: not wearing makeup, not doing my hair, or wearing pjs around the house. She would still stop and just look at me and say, "You are so beautiful." She saw my heart and saw me for me, and I couldn't be more thankful for the mother-in-law that I was given.

Even though she also has another daughter, she treated me like I was not just an "in-law". She would say, "Cher you're really a daughter to me." She also always had my back, even when it came to telling her son how to best treat a lady. She was so open, honest, caring, including, and her warm heart is what made our bond one that lasts forever. I am so thankful for all her words of wisdom, guidance, love, and devotion.

I will always love Amy Gopman, my mother-in-law and biggest inspiration.

So to you all, I say, embrace less traditional, mother-daughter relationships. They can be just as rewarding and truly change your life!

Stepmothers and Stepdaughters

Relationships between stepmothers and their stepdaughters are famously difficult to manage. But, despite what Cinderella might have experienced, we're here to tell you that with some effort and good intentions, this type of relationship can truly blossom into something wonderful and unique.

One of the key things for stepmoms to remember is that, in many cases, stepdaughters already have a mother who they love and who loves them dearly. It's very important to let your stepdaughter know that you aren't trying to take the place of their mother, and that you too can have a loving relationship without it being a betrayal of the bond they have with their mother. Another concern that was brought up in our discussions with stepdaughters is the fear that their fathers will no longer put them first now that the stepmother is on the scene. Don't be afraid to get all those feelings out in the open, and do your best not to internalize them. As the new "parental" figure in their lives, setting aside ego for the greater good will make all the difference. Loving their mother and even mourning the loss of the family life they knew is not a rejection of you. You can still create your own family, with your own new traditions and a relationship full of love that is every bit as rich as a mother-daughter relationship. Have patience. Don't force things or try to buy her love. Instead, apply constant, unwavering support. Make sure that she feels special and listened to. Show with your actions that you don't intend to dominate the family dynamic, and that your presence isn't meant to subtract from the family. In fact, your goal is to add even more love to your little tribe.

Nevertheless, don't overdo it. Big, sweeping gestures and quick changes will only make her put her guard up and resist. Instead, let things unfold at a more natural pace. Talk to her about what she likes or doesn't like and put small changes into action slowly over time. Similar to traditional mother-daughter relationships, make sure to make special time for your stepdaughter. Don't treat her as a burden or foreign person in your life. Instead treat her as a valued family member who you want to get close with and support.

No matter how hard you try, there's always a chance she may rebel at first. Age often plays a factor here, as does the nature of the relationship between the parents. An adversarial relationship between her mother and father and/or lingering feelings of bitterness can make this difficult. That said, if you stay consistent, show her you care, and refrain from speaking poorly of her mother, she will eventually see you as a positive addition to the family. You are now married (or soon to be) and have a loving partner. Appreciate that relationship and remember that his children are an integral part of that relationship. Putting in the work to ensure that your partner knows how much you value their children will not just benefit you and your stepdaughter. It will also strengthen your relationship with your spouse and create a more stable environment for all of the children in these blended families.

On the other side of the coin, as a stepdaughter, it's important to take the time to really get to know your new family member.

We understand that this change can be very tough, but remember that your parent chose her for a reason. Your parent found something special in her. Try to find that specialness, too. Most of all, remember that she does not have to take the place of your biological mom, but she can be a new role model or friend in your life, and caring for her isn't a betrayal of your mother.

Another helpful viewpoint might be to remember that your parent is happy in this new marriage. Be happy for them! If you allow change into your life, it can be positive and rewarding. Give them a chance!

But remember that it does take time. Most likely your new stepmom feels the same way you do. Nervous that she might say or do the wrong thing. Maybe she even feels threatened or fearful that you'll hate her. Instead of just looking at her as your stepmom, view her as a human being. A woman who is embarking on a whole new journey without a map. Keep in mind that it isn't easy coming into an established family and trying to fit in! Treat her as you would a new potential friend. Be kind, courteous, generous, and open to the possibilities. If she does the same, you might find that you've been blessed with a truly special relationship that you wouldn't trade for the world!

Single Mothers

We have a special space in our hearts for single mothers. This is a unique life situation because not only does this mother have to play the role of mom, but also as sole provider. It's harder for a single mother to divide her time equally between the things she has to do, and the things she wants to do. This mother wants to have a strong relationship with her daughter, but she also knows she has to keep working in order to afford the simplest of things to survive. Oftentimes, the hours of the day are spent on doing what is necessary to continue maintaining a healthy life, and spending time with your daughter may be pushed onto the back burner until that mother has more time.

To single mothers, we understand how difficult life must be for your unique situation. There will come a time where your daughter will look back on her younger years and see all you sacrificed in order to provide everything you could for your family. As the days, weeks, months, and years pass by, just try to do little things each day to remind your daughter that you are there for her.

After reading this book, we hope you see that it is still possible to nurture a mother-daughter relationship, even if you don't have a lot of time or resources. All you have to do is continue trying your best and showing your daughter how much you are dedicated to her in every way that you can.

Daughters of single mothers, try not to be too hard or demanding of your mother. We know it might be hard to see sometimes, especially if she always seems to be working and spending less time with you, but believe that she is truly doing all of that *for* you and it comes from a place of pure and selfless love. Help your mother any way that you can, even if it's taking the time to talk to her about your day and then asking more details about hers. Get in the kitchen and surprise her with a meal when she gets home from work so you can eat together and talk. Little things really do add up!

"I am not a perfect mother and I will never be. You are not a perfect daughter and you will never be. But put us together and we will be the best mother and daughter we would ever be." – Zoraida Pesante

In closing, to all mothers and daughters reading this book, remember that focusing and taking action is the key to maintaining or creating a strong connection. No matter the current condition of your relationship (barring abuse and toxic behavior) or how you came to be a mother or daughter, there is nothing holding you back from having the relationship of your dreams besides *your* own unwillingness to try. We know what it takes to have a strong relationship, and we know how effortless it can be if we love each other and strive to *express* that love to each other.

No more excuses!

Close this book, take that first step, and go love your mother or daughter like you've never done before.

Author Bios

Dawn Hubsher is a bubbly, charismatic and strong minded woman who believes in living life to the fullest. She's been married to Dr. Mason I. Hubsher for 36 years and has 3 grown children. She is a firm believer in finding your inner happiness and feels that a strong family bond is one of life's greatest joys!

Dawn has worn many hats over the years, first supporting her husband through medical school with her job as a dental hygienist, then as a mother to their young children, and now as the administrator of his successful medical practice. She's a big proponent of mindful giving and supports as many charitable organizations as she can.

When Dawn isn't busy with her job and charity work, she can be found twinning with Cher, shopping all the newest trends, or beasting in the gym.

Cher Hubsher (Gopman) is happily married to her college sweetheart, Dr. Jared M. Gopman, and currently resides in New York City. Her first major foray into television began with MTV, where her birthday bash was featured on My Super Sweet 16. The reality TV journey continued with a second show called Exiled, where she was sent to the jungles of Panama to stay with the Embera tribe.

Since her MTV days, Cher has worked in a number of different fields, becoming a professional cheerleader, an actress (with parts in movies like 'Inoperable' and 'Amityville Terror'), and later, a registered nurse. Her nursing journey began in mental health, but later turned to cosmetic medical procedures.

Unable to tame her entrepreneurial spirit and her passion for helping people fall in love, Cher went on to open her own boutique date coaching company called NYC Wingwoman.

Cher and her mother have always been extremely close and, when an opportunity came their way to feature their relationship on television, they figured, "Why not?" Cher couldn't wait to show the world that it was cool to be close with your mom!

When Cher isn't busy matchmaking/coaching in Manhattan, she can be found planning matching outfits for her and her daughter to wear when she enters the world, and dreaming of the day she can have her own animal sanctuary.

Want to stay connected with this amazing mother-daughter duo? Follow Dawn and Cher's escapades on TLC's new series, 'sMothered' and check out their website at www.abondthatlastsforever.com!

If you enjoyed this book, please leave an online review. As a thank you, send us a screenshot to abondthatlastsforever@gmail.com, and we will send you an autographed personalized note back!

Note from the Authors

We have tried to recreate events, locales and conversations as best we could from our memories of them. In some instances, though, we made a conscious choice to change the names of individuals, places, and some identifying characteristics in order to protect the anonymity of the parties involved.